WEBER'S
MEDITERRANEAN
BARBECUE

WEBER'S
MEDITERRANEAN
BARBECUE

BRING THE TASTE OF THE SUN TO YOUR BARBECUE
WITH MORE THAN 100 FRESH AND TASTY RECIPES

JAMIE PURVIANCE

hamlyn

CONTENTS

INTRODUCTION

Close your eyes. Imagine you're sitting at a beachside restaurant while the warm, blue sea laps along the shore gently and aromas of rosemary and oregano drift from a smoky grill outside the kitchen. A waiter sets down a plate of sizzling, seared veal chops with buttery orzo tossed with baby spinach and lemon. There are grill-roasted tomatoes, too, and a glass of silky, smooth wine at your table.

Under the Mediterranean sun, dining al fresco like this takes place naturally because the climate is so mild and welcoming. In fact, in many parts around here people spend much of their lives outside: on shaded patios, under vine-decked arbours, and right along the beach. It's a lifestyle a lot of us want to visit and revisit, year after year. But, of course, we can't all be there all the time. So, the next best thing is recreating that type of experience in our homes.

This is a book about opening doors and turning your outdoor space into a little corner of the Mediterranean. That starts with the food, of course, and there are so many spectacular options. Do your favourite dishes come from Spain – perhaps a colourful seafood paella or a fish stew made rich with grilled sausages and vegetables? Or maybe your tastes lean toward Italy – the land of luscious mushroom risottos and grilled pizzas topped with bubbling cheeses.

In France, chicken is pounded thin to soak up the earthy flavours of fresh herbs and live fires, and then jumbled with salty capers and the Mediterranean's ubiquitous fruit: lemon.

In Greece they adore their grilled meats – especially lamb – paired with mint, garlic and peppery olive oil – a combination that will reward you over and over for very little time and effort. In this book, we also journey to Portugal for a chorizo-studded caldo verde, as well as Morocco, where lifting the lid of a tagine reveals exotic aromas and brilliant colours. Here in the Mediterranean you can even bring dessert outdoors, roasting oranges in foil and imbuing them with the liquorice flavours of ouzo and the warmth of cinnamon. Or maybe you would prefer to grill soft, ripe plums and top them with a spiced butter spiked with brandy.

The techniques in this book are wonderfully simple. Following the recipes, you will see how easy it is to add smoky, charred flavours to a range of local ingredients available at most good supermarkets. Moving your cooking – and ideally, dining – outside makes the biggest difference between boring and memorable meals. Just as the food all across the Mediterranean, from the beach bars of Nice to the pizzerias of Naples, is honest and comforting, so are the recipes here. No matter where you are now, you have access to the specialities of this place. On any given day you can bring home the flavours and spirit of this venerated region.

Jamie Purviance

STARTING A CHARCOAL GRILL

Got a match? You and your charcoal grill, right? All jokes aside, plan on carving out 15–20 minutes to get your fire going.

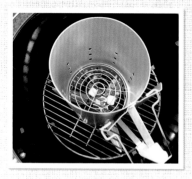

1. LIFE'S EASIER WITH A CHIMNEY STARTER. This metal cylinder with a wire rack and handles gets the fire going quickly. Simply fill the cylinder with charcoal briquettes, and then place some wadded-up newspaper or lighter cubes on the charcoal grate under the chimney starter.

2. LIGHT, CHIMNEY, ACTION. Once you light the newspaper or lighter cubes, the briquettes will fire up with little risk of a flameout. You'll see the chimney smoking at first, but don't make a move until the top coals are covered in white ash.

3. GLOVES ON. Wearing insulated barbecue mitts, grab both of the chimney handles and carefully pour the hot coals on to the charcoal grate. That swinging handle is designed to make it safer and easier to aim the coals.

4. COAL PLAY. We like the flexibility of a two-zone fire, where all the coals are pushed to one side of the charcoal grate, providing an area that will give you a 'safety zone' – a place to temporarily move food if it begins to flare up over direct heat.

5. JUST ABOUT GO TIME. Put the cooking grate back in place, and cover the grill with the lid. In 10–15 minutes, the temperature of the grill should be close to 260°C /500°F. This is when you want to brush the grate clean with a stainless-steel grill brush.

6. MAKE SURE THE TOP AND BOTTOM VENTS ARE OPEN. While grilling, the vent on the bottom half of the grill should be wide open and clear of ashes, to provide enough air for the fire. Keep the vent on the top open as well, unless you want to lower the temperature a bit by closing the top vent about halfway.

STARTING A GAS GRILL

Skills required: lid lifting and knob turning. The huge advantage of gas grilling is its ease, but there are a few important tips to follow:

1. FIRST THINGS FIRST. Lift the lid, and then check to make sure you have enough fuel. Replace your cylinder if it's empty or near empty to ensure you have enough fuel to get you through your entire cook time. Also check the grease tray and clean if needed.

2. LIGHT THE GRILL. Follow your Owner's Guide for lighting and leak test instructions. If you smell gas, that might indicate a leak around the connection or in the hose. Turn off all the burners. Close the valves on your cylinder and disconnect the hose. Wait 5–10 minutes, and then reconnect the hose. Try lighting the grill again. If you still smell gas, shut the grill down and call the manufacturer.

3. GRILL ON, LID GOES DOWN. Close the lid and wait 10–15 minutes for the grill to preheat. This creates the oven-like environment needed for efficient cooking and gets the cooking grates good and hot for the perfect sear. It also makes the grates much easier to clean.

DIRECT AND INDIRECT COOKING

It's time for us to be direct – and indirect – regarding heat.

There are two basic ways of grilling your food: directly over hot coals or fired-up burners, or indirectly, where the heat is on both sides of the food. Direct cooking doles out a hefty blast of heat, which gives food that satisfying, crunchy sear, while indirect heat is gentler, transforming the grill into an oven that cooks your meal more gradually.

Direct heat is best used when grilling thinner, tender items that cook quickly: think steak, chops, boneless chicken pieces, fish fillets, shellfish, cut vegetables and fruit.

Indirect heat is the way to go for larger, tougher cuts of meat that take a while to cook, such as bone-in chicken pieces and legs of lamb.

In many cases, we like to dabble in both types of heat to achieve a good external crust with the preferred internal doneness level to match. This approach leads to more dependable outcomes and not as many awkward 'surprise – it's raw!' moments at the dinner table. To ensure tasty success, start your item over direct heat to sear on both sides, and then move it to the indirect zone to finish up without getting torched. You'll need to build an indirect fire for this, where the hot coals are divided equally on both sides of the charcoal grate and the centre of the grate is empty, or where some of the burners are turned off on a gas grill.

In order for all this direct-indirect stuff to work, you need to know that the lid is your friend. Keeping it closed as much as possible is what retains the swirling radiant heat you need for indirect cooking, as well as prevents flare-ups in direct use. You'll still need to turn your food, but when the heat can cook the food from the top and bottom simultaneously, grilling tends to go much faster, which, of course, means the eating part arrives more quickly.

CHARCOAL: DIRECT COOKING
With direct heat, the fire is right below the food. The heat radiates off the charcoal and conducts through the metal cooking grate to create those dark, handsome grill marks.

CHARCOAL: INDIRECT COOKING
With indirect heat, the charcoal is arranged on both sides of the food.

GAS: DIRECT AND INDIRECT COOKING
Using direct heat on a gas grill is simply a matter of grilling the food right over lit burners. To use indirect heat, light the burners on the far left and far right of the grill, and grill the food over the unlit burner(s) between them. If your grill has just two burners, light one of them and grill over the unlit one for indirect cooking.

GRILL MAINTENANCE/SAFETY

Outdoorsy types tend to be pretty low maintenance – grills included. That said, embracing a couple of simple upkeep rituals can keep your grill going, and going strong, for a very long time.

To achieve the coveted grill marks, keep food from sticking, and eliminate the chances of old burnt barnacles on your food, the cooking grates need to be cleaned before every use. Close the lid and preheat your grill to about 260°C/500°F for 10 minutes. Slip your hand into an insulated barbecue mitt and use a long-handled grill brush to do a quick once-over of the grates, dislodging any charred bits left behind from past meals. That quick treatment does the trick.

Keep your grill in tip-top, efficient shape by giving it a more thorough cleaning every month or so. Check the instructions in your Owner's Guide, but start by wiping down the outside of your grill with warm, soapy water. Scrape any accumulated debris from the inside of the lid. Gas grillers should remove the cooking grates, brush the burners, and clean out the bottom of the cook box and drip pan. Charcoal grillers should regularly remove all ash sitting at the bottom of the kettle.

Check your Owner's Guide to get the full report on the ultimate deep clean, upkeep and maintenance for your grill.

GRILL SAFETY

Please read your Owner's Guide and familiarise yourself with and follow all 'dangers', 'warnings' and 'cautions'. Also follow the grilling procedures and maintenance requirements listed in your Owner's Guide. If you cannot locate the Owner's Guide for your grill model, please contact the manufacturer prior to use. If you have any questions concerning the 'dangers', 'warnings' and 'cautions' contained in your Weber® gas, charcoal or electric grill Owner's Guide, or if you do not have an Owner's Guide for your specific grill model, please visit www.weber.com to access your Owner's Guide before using your grill.

A sturdy grill brush with stainless-steel bristles is essential for cleaning your cooking grate. A notched scraper on the grill head is especially good at loosening hardened bits.

11

PIZZA STONE

A good pizza stone produces an evenly light and crispy crust and guarantees that your creation remains on, not under, the cooking grates.

DISPOSABLE FOIL TRAYS

Available in a variety of sizes, disposable foil trays offer many conveniences. Use them to move food to and from the grill and to keep food warm on the cooking grates.

BARBECUE GLOVES

Choose gloves that are insulated and that cover both hands and wrists.

CHIMNEY STARTER

This is the simplest tool for starting charcoal faster and more evenly than you ever could with lighter fuel. Look for one with a capacity of at least 5 litres.

INSTANT-READ THERMOMETER

Small and relatively inexpensive, this gadget is essential for quickly gauging the internal temperature of the meat when grilling.

TONGS

Definitely the hardest working tool of all. You will need three pairs: one for raw food, one for cooked food and one for arranging charcoal.

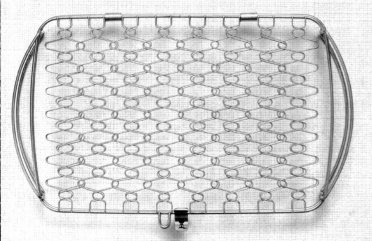

FISH BASKET

Great for grilling whole fish, a fish basket makes it easier to turn the fish and lift it off the grate slightly so you don't leave any behind on the grill when you turn.

SPATULA

Look for a long-handled spatula designed with a bent (offset) neck so that the blade is set lower than the handle. This makes it easier to lift food off the cooking grates.

GRILL BRUSH

A must-use before you even dream of grilling. A quick once-over on hot grates prevents the charred remains of meals past from sticking to your meals present.

SKEWERS

It is always fun to eat food on a stick. Look for skewers with wide, flat sides or double prongs to prevent ingredients from spinning on the skewers as you turn them over.

MAKING FLATBREADS

People have been making flatbreads outside since the dawn of civilisation. Draping thin rounds of dough over a hot stone set by a smouldering fire was probably the first method. Wood-fired ovens came along later and produced even better results. Those blazing hot ovens are still popular today throughout the Mediterranean region, but it turns out that a grill does an excellent job of achieving many of the same flavours and textures you would get from a wood-fired oven.

1 MAKE YOUR OWN DOUGH

There are at least a few ways to make dough for flatbreads and pizzas: by hand, with a stand mixer, or with a food processor. The easier and quickest way uses a food processor fitted with a plastic dough blade. Process the dough until it forms a ball that rides on top of the blade. It should be soft but not sticky.

2 ROLL IT THINLY

To roll dough into a thin crust, it needs to be relaxed; otherwise, the dough tends to spring back when you stretch it. Let the dough sit at room temperature for about an hour. Then you should be able to roll it out easily with a rolling pin or stretch it with your hands. If it continues to spring back, let the dough relax a bit longer at room temperature.

3 CHOOSE YOUR TOOL

There are a few options for getting the dough to the grill. The best is on a pizza paddle, either metal or wooden. You can also use the underside of a baking sheet. One other possibility is to drape it over a rolling pin and hold it in place.

4 LET IT SLIDE

Flour is the key to whatever tool you use for sliding your dough on to the pizza stone. The tiny granules of flour help the dough slip easily on and off the paddle. Don't use cornmeal, as some cookbooks recommend. It tends to burn on the hot stone, creating an unpleasant taste in the dough.

5 PICK YOUR TOPPINGS

Less is more when it comes to pizza and flatbreads. Choose your favourites and top your dough, leaving around a 1 cm/½ inch gap at the edges to allow a crust to form. One wonderful combination includes roasted garlic, mozzarella cheese, charred tenderstem broccoli and peppers, and a sprinkling of pecorino cheese (for recipe, see page 148).

6 TOAST AND TURN

Always remember to preheat your pizza stone for about 15 minutes before sliding the dough on top. When the moist dough hits the hot stone, the water inside turns to gas and creates a bunch of bubbles that lift the dough and create air pockets for a light, crispy texture. After your pizza or flatbread has been cooking for a couple of minutes, rotate it on the stone to ensure an even bake. After a few minutes the toppings will be bubbling and your dough will have a nice cripsy stone baked finish.

GRILLING KEBABS

Something good almost always happens when you cook skewered meat over an open fire. To get your best results each time, keep these fundamentals in mind. As long as these are part of your plan, you can play around with various types of skewers, various types of meats and vegetables, and other fun touches, like special sauces and glazes.

1 SKEWERS

Skewers come in metal or wooden varieties. Both work well. The metal ones are reusable, but that, of course, means you need to clean them after the meal is done. The wooden ones are inexpensive and disposable, but you need to soak them in water first to prevent them from burning.

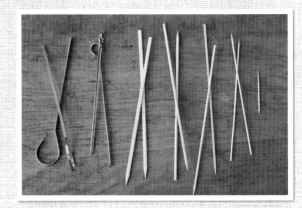

2 MEAT

Don't make the common mistake of putting just any meat on skewers. The grilling time is almost always so short that you should start with meat that is naturally tender and juicy. For example, with pork, use nicely marbled meat from the loin or fillet. If you don't see those whole pieces at the shop, buy pork chops and cut the meat into chunks that are each about the same size and thickness.

3 THE METHOD

Flat-sided skewers are nice because they hold your meat and vegetables in place when you turn the skewers. If you don't have any of those, use the thickest skewers possible or use two thin skewers arranged side by side. For the meat to cook evenly, leave a little bit of room between the pieces. It's OK if the edges touch, but if the pieces are crammed together, the meat will take longer to cook and it might get dry.

4 SHAPE UP AND CHILL OUT

Another good option for kebabs is to use minced meat. That way you can flavour the meat however you like and you are almost guaranteed tender results. Portion the meat into loosely packed little mounds first. Then gently form each mound around the top end of a skewer, leaving a few centimetres of skewer bare near the tip. Grilling minced meat kebabs right away runs the risk of the meat falling apart. Instead, line up the skewers on a roasting tray, cover the tray with clingfilm and refrigerate for 1–2 hours. That time in the refrigerator helps a great deal to firm up the meat so that it holds together well on the grill.

5 SHIELD THE WOOD

Soaking bamboo skewers in water for 30 minutes or so should prevent them from catching fire, but still the wood sometimes turns black and disintegrates on the grill. So, make a shield by folding a large sheet of aluminium foil in half to create a long rectangle. Lay the shield on the front edge of the cooking grate and lay each skewer on top so that most of the exposed wood is protected from direct heat.

APPETISERS

ARTICHOKES

WITH LEMON, GARLIC AND PARMESAN

PREP TIME: 15 minutes, plus 25–30 minutes to steam the artichokes

GRILLING TIME: 16–18 minutes

75 ml/3 fl oz extra-virgin olive oil
4 tablespoons fresh lemon juice
1 garlic clove, finely chopped
½ teaspoon coarse salt
1 tablespoon finely chopped flat-leaf parsley
½ teaspoon finely grated lemon zest
1 lemon, cut in half
2 large artichokes
2 tablespoons finely grated Parmesan cheese

1 Whisk the oil, lemon juice, garlic and salt. Pour off 4 tablespoons for basting the artichokes. Add the parsley and lemon zest to the remaining oil for use after grilling.

2 Fill a saucepan with 5 cm/2 inches of water. Trim the stalks of the artichoke and cut off the sharp leaf tips with kitchen scissors. Rub the artichokes all over with a lemon half, and then squeeze the remaining lemon juice from the half into the water. Place the artichokes, stalks down, into the water. Bring to the boil, and then cover and reduce the heat to medium-low. Steam the artichokes until the bottoms are easily pierced with a knife, 25–30 minutes, depending on their size. Remove from the saucepan and transfer to a bowl of iced water to stop the cooking. When cool enough to handle, drain well, cut the artichokes lengthways in half, and scrape out the chokes and small purple leaves with a spoon. Brush the artichokes with some of the basting oil.

3 Prepare the grill for direct and indirect cooking over medium heat (180–230°C/350–450°F).

4 Grill the artichokes over **grilling/direct medium heat** for about 8 minutes, with the lid closed, until charred on both sides, turning as needed. Slide over **roasting/indirect medium heat** and continue to cook for 8–10 minutes more, until very tender, basting with the oil and turning once or twice. During the last minute of grilling time, turn the artichokes cut side up, and top with the cheese to melt.

5 Transfer the artichokes to a serving plate and drizzle with some of the garlic oil. Serve warm or at room temperature with the remaining garlic oil.

SERVES: 4

CORN ON THE COB

WITH BASIL-PARMESAN BUTTER

PREP TIME: 10 minutes
GRILLING TIME: 10–15 minutes

BUTTER

50 g/2 oz unsalted butter, softened
25 g/1 oz freshly grated Parmesan cheese
2 tablespoons finely chopped basil
½ teaspoon sea salt
¼ teaspoon ground black pepper
¼ teaspoon granules garlic

2 corn on the cobs, husked

1 Prepare the grill for direct cooking over medium heat (180–230°C/350–450°F).

2 In a small bowl mash the butter ingredients with the back of a fork, and then stir to distribute the seasonings throughout the butter.

3 Brush about 1 tablespoon of the seasoned butter all over each corn cob. Brush the cooking grates clean. Grill the corn over **grilling/direct medium heat** for 10–15 minutes, with the lid closed as much as possible, until browned in spots and tender, turning occasionally. Serve warm with the remaining butter spread on the corn.

SERVES: 4

GAZPACHO

WITH ROASTED PEPPERS AND ALMONDS

PREP TIME: 15 minutes
GRILLING TIME: 10–20 minutes
CHILLING TIME: 2–4 hours

3 plum tomatoes
1 onion, cut crossways into 1-cm/½-inch slices
1 red pepper
1 green pepper

SOUP

1 cucumber, roughly chopped
2 garlic cloves
500 ml/17 fl oz tomato juice
4 tablespoons fresh lime juice
4 tablespoons roughly chopped flat-leaf parsley
2 tablespoons extra-virgin olive oil
2 teaspoons coarse salt
1 teaspoon hot pepper sauce, or to taste
1 teaspoon ground cumin
1 teaspoon paprika
½ teaspoon freshly ground black pepper

4 tablespoons almonds, toasted and roughly chopped
Finely chopped flat-leaf parsley

1 Prepare the grill for direct cooking over medium heat (180–230°C /350–450°F).

2 Grill the tomatoes, onion and peppers over **grilling/ direct medium heat** , with the lid closed, until the tomatoes are charred on all sides, 6–8 minutes; the onion is tender, 8–10 minutes; and the peppers are blackened and blistered all over, 10–20 minutes, turning as needed. Remove from the grill as they are done.

3 When cool enough to handle, peel away the charred skin and remove the seeds from the tomatoes. Put the peppers in a bowl and cover with clingfilm to trap the steam. Let stand for about 10 minutes. Remove from the bowl and peel away and discard the charred skin. Cut off and discard the stalks and seeds, and coarsely chop.

4 Put the tomatoes, onion, peppers, cucumber and garlic in the bowl of a food processor and process until coarsely chopped. Add the remaining soup ingredients and process until blended but slightly chunky. Cover and refrigerate for 2–4 hours.

5 Ladle the gazpacho into bowls and serve garnished with the almonds and parsley.

SERVES: 4

BABA GANOUSH

PREP TIME: 15 minutes
GRILLING TIME: about 32 minutes

2 large aubergines, each about 500 g/1 lb
2 garlic cloves, finely chopped
4 tablespoons fresh lemon juice
2 tablespoons tahini
1 teaspoon coarse salt
½ teaspoon ground cumin
¼ teaspoon freshly ground black pepper
⅛ teaspoon ground cayenne pepper
2 tablespoons finely chopped flat-leaf parsley
2 tablespoons extra-virgin olive oil

1 Prepare the grill for direct and indirect cooking over medium heat (180–230°C /350–450°F).

2 Pierce the aubergines all over with a fork approximately 10 times, and then grill over **grilling/direct medium heat** for about 12 minutes, with the lid closed, until the skin is charred, turning as needed. Move the aubergines over **roasting/indirect medium heat** and continue to cook until very soft and beginning to collapse, about 20 minutes more. Remove from the grill and, when cool enough to handle, cut open the aubergines and scoop the pulp into the bowl of a food processor. Discard the skins.

3 Add the garlic, lemon juice, tahini, salt, cumin, pepper and cayenne to the food processor and pulse five to six times to form a slightly chunky consistency. Add the parsley and 1 tablespoon of the oil and pulse one to two times to blend. Scoop the dip into a serving bowl and drizzle with the remaining 1 tablespoon oil. Serve with pitta bread or baguette pieces.

MAKES: about 500 ml/17 fl oz

TIROSALATA DIP

WITH GRILLED PITTA WEDGES

PREP TIME: 15 minutes
GRILLING TIME: 8–12 minutes

2 jalapeño chillies
1 garlic clove, chopped
Extra-virgin olive oil
1/2 teaspoon finely grated lemon zest
1 tablespoon fresh lemon juice
Coarse salt
1/4 teaspoon freshly ground black pepper
175 g/6 oz feta cheese, crumbled
125 g/4 oz full-fat Greek yogurt
2 large pitta breads, each cut into 8 wedges and then
     separated into 2 pieces

NOTE!

This tangy feta dip is a popular appetiser served in Greece. Roasted jalapeño chillies infuse the creamy blend of feta and yogurt with smoky heat and peppery flavour. If possible, choose a creamier feta versus a crumbly version for a smooth dip.

1 Prepare the grill for direct cooking over medium heat (180–230°C /350–450°F).

2 Grill the chillies over **grilling/direct medium heat** for 6–8 minutes, with the lid closed, until the skins are blackened and blistered all over, turning once or twice. Set aside to cool. Cut off and discard the stems and seeds, and then roughly chop the chillies.

3 Place the chillies, garlic, 4 tablespoons oil, lemon zest and juice, 1/2 teaspoon salt, and pepper in a food processor and process until blended. Add the feta and yogurt and process until smooth. Transfer to a serving bowl.

4 Brush the pitta wedges with oil and lightly season with salt. Grill over **grilling/direct medium heat** for 2–4 minutes, with the lid closed, until toasted, turning once.

5 Serve the dip at room temperature with the pitta wedges.

MAKES: about 250–350 ml/8–12 fl oz

SERRANO HAM-WRAPPED FIGS

STUFFED WITH GOATS' CHEESE

PREP TIME: 10 minutes
GRILLING TIME: 8–12 minutes
SPECIAL EQUIPMENT: 8 cocktail sticks

8 firm but ripe, medium to large fresh figs, stalks trimmed
65 g/2½ oz soft goats' cheese
8 thin slices Serrano ham
100 g/3½ oz baby rocket
Extra-virgin olive oil
Balsamic vinegar
Freshly ground black pepper

1 Prepare the grill for indirect cooking over medium-high heat (as close to 220°C /425°F as possible).

2 Make a small 'x' incision in the top of each fig. Gently and partially open the fig and push about 2 teaspoons goats' cheese into the centre. Press the top to close. Wipe away any cheese that may be left on the outside of the fig. Wrap each fig crossways with a ham slice, and then insert a cocktail stick through the fig to secure the ham.

3 Grill the figs, stalk side up, over **roasting/indirect medium-high heat** for 8–12 minutes, with the lid closed, until the ham begins to crisp and the cheese begins to melt.

4 Scatter the rocket on a serving plate. Place the figs on the rocket and remove the cocktail sticks. Lightly drizzle the figs and rocket with oil and a few drops of vinegar. Garnish with black pepper. Serve immediately.

SERVES: 4–8

GARLICKY BRUSCHETTA 🍴

WITH BASIL OIL, PEPPERS AND MOZZARELLA

PREP TIME: 25 minutes
GRILLING TIME: 13–19 minutes

15 g/½ oz fresh basil leaves
75 ml/3 fl oz extra-virgin olive oil
1 garlic clove, finely chopped
Coarse salt
Freshly ground black pepper
2 red peppers, each about 175 g/6 oz
4 slices artisan bread, each about 1 cm/½ inch thick, cut crossways in half
2 garlic cloves, peeled and cut in half
250 g/8 oz mozzarella cheese, cut into 5-mm/¼-inch slices

1 Prepare the grill for direct and indirect cooking over medium heat (180–230°C /350–450°F).

2 In a mini food processor combine the basil, oil, garlic, ¼ teaspoon salt and ⅛ teaspoon pepper. Blend thoroughly, stopping the machine to scrape down the inside of the bowl once or twice.

3 Grill the peppers over **grilling/direct medium heat** for 10–12 minutes, with the lid closed, until blackened and blistered all over, turning occasionally. Transfer to a bowl and cover with clingfilm to trap the steam. Allow to stand for about 10 minutes. Remove and discard the charred skin, stalks, and seeds and cut the peppers into 5-mm/¼-inch strips. Place the peppers in a bowl. Add 2 tablespoons of the basil oil and stir to coat.

4 Grill the bread over **grilling/direct medium heat** for about 1 minute, with the lid closed, until golden on the bottom side (do not turn). Remove the bread from the grill, rub the toasted side with the cut side of the garlic, lightly season with salt, arrange the cheese slices on top, and lightly season with salt and pepper.

5 Grill the bread, cheese side up, over **roasting/indirect medium heat** for 1–2 minutes, with the lid closed, until the cheese begins to melt. Transfer to a serving plate and spoon the peppers over the cheese. Drizzle with the remaining basil oil. Serve immediately.

SERVES: 4

MIXED GRILLED VEGETABLES

ON GOATS' CHEESE TOASTS

PREP TIME: 20 minutes
GRILLING TIME: about 14 minutes

2 green or yellow courgettes, about 375 g/12 oz total, cut
    lengthways into 5-mm/¼-inch slices
1 aubergine, about 375 g/12 oz, cut crossways into 5-mm/
    ¼-inch slices
1 red or yellow pepper, about 300 g/10 oz, cut into 4 sections
Extra-virgin olive oil
1¼ teaspoons coarse salt
¾ teaspoon freshly ground black pepper
1 loaf French bread, about 425 g/14 oz, cut into 1-cm/½-inch
    thick slices
2 garlic cloves, each peeled and cut in half
250 g/8 oz soft goats' cheese (chèvre), at room temperature
2 tablespoons finely chopped mint

1 Prepare the grill for direct cooking over medium-high heat
(200–230°C/400–450°F).

2 Lightly brush the vegetables on both sides with oil and
season evenly with the salt and pepper. Working in
batches, if necessary, grill the vegetables over **grilling/direct
medium-high heat**, with the lid closed, until nicely marked
from the grill, turning as needed. The courgettes will take about
4 minutes, the aubergine will take about 10 minutes, and the
pepper will take 12–14 minutes. Remove the vegetables from
the grill as they are done, and cut into bite-sized pieces.

3 Brush each slice of bread on one side with a little oil, and
then grill, oiled side down, over **grilling/direct medium-
high heat** for 30 seconds–1 minute, with the lid closed, until
golden brown (do not turn). Rub the grilled side of the bread
with the cut side of the garlic, and spread the cheese evenly
on the toasts. Drizzle the vegetables lightly with oil and spoon
generously on to the toasts. Garnish with mint.

SERVES: 6

FILO PARCELS

STUFFED WITH BRIE AND GRAPES

PREP TIME: 40 minutes
GRILLING TIME: 8–11 minutes
SPECIAL EQUIPMENT: perforated grill pan

6 spring onions, ends trimmed
Extra-virgin olive oil
Coarse salt
Freshly ground black pepper
150 g/5 oz seedless grapes, each cut in half
50 g/2 oz sultanas
12 sheets frozen filo pastry, thawed
Plain flour
200 g/7 oz partially frozen Brie cheese, rind removed and
    cheese cut into thin slices
1 egg white, lightly beaten with a pinch of salt

1 Prepare the grill for direct and indirect cooking over medium-high heat (200–230°C/400–450°F) and preheat a perforated grill pan over direct heat.

2 Lightly brush the spring onions with oil, season with a pinch of salt and pepper, and then grill on the grill pan over **grilling/direct medium-high heat** for 3–4 minutes, with the lid closed, until charred and slightly tender, turning once. Coarsely chop. Slide the grill pan over indirect heat.

3 In a small bowl combine the spring onions, grapes and sultanas. Place one sheet of filo pastry on a lightly floured board and brush all over with a light coating of oil. Fold lengthways in half, two times. Place 1 rounded tablespoon of the grape mixture at the bottom, short end, leaving a 2.5-cm/1-inch border on either long side; top with 15 g/½ oz of the Brie. Brush all the edges of the filo sheet with the egg white. Fold into a triangle, starting at the bottom short end and folding towards the top, enclosing the filling completely. Press the edges to seal securely, brushing with a little egg white as needed. Place the parcel on a baking sheet. Repeat with the remaining filo sheets and filling. Lightly brush the tops with oil.

4 Grill the filo parcels on the grill pan over **roasting/indirect medium-high heat** for 5–6 minutes, with the lid closed, until golden and crisp. Transfer to a serving plate and serve warm.

SERVES: 4–6

MOZZARELLA AND ROSEMARY SKEWERS

WITH PARMA HAM AND BASIL

PREP TIME: 20 minutes
GRILLING TIME: 3–4 minutes
SPECIAL EQUIPMENT: perforated grill pan

24 fresh rosemary sprigs, each 7–10 cm/3–4 inches long, or cocktail sticks
24 bite-sized mozzarella balls, 250 g/8 oz total, drained
1 teaspoon freshly ground black pepper
24 medium basil leaves
8 thin slices Parma ham, each cut lengthways into thirds
Extra-virgin olive oil spray
1 small lemon, cut crossways in half

1 Preheat the grill for indirect cooking over high heat (230–290°C /450–550°F) and preheat a perforated grill pan.

2 Strip off the green leaves from about 3.5 cm/1½ inches of the blunt end of the rosemary sprigs, leaving some leaves on the other end. Roll each mozzarella ball in the pepper. Wrap a basil leaf around each mozzarella ball, and then cover each with a strip of ham, overlapping and enclosing the cheese completely. Thread each ball on a rosemary sprig, starting at the stripped end of the rosemary.

3 Spray the rosemary leaves with olive oil spray to help them from turning black and crumbly on the grill. Place the skewers in a single layer on the grill pan and grill over **roasting/indirect high heat** for 3–4 minutes, with the lid closed, until the cheese is softened but not completely melted and the ham looks barely golden. (You may have to grill the skewers in batches.) Transfer to a serving plate and squeeze the lemon on top. Serve warm.

SERVES: 4–6

POLENTA

WITH SAUSAGE AND SUN-DRIED TOMATO RAGU

PREP TIME: 15 minutes, plus about 30 minutes for the ragu
STANDING TIME: 1 hour
GRILLING TIME: 6–8 minutes

275 g/9 oz instant polenta
500 ml/17 fl oz vegetable stock or chicken stock
250 ml/8 fl oz full-fat milk
1 tablespoon extra-virgin olive oil
375 g/12 oz fresh Italian sausages, hot or mild, casings removed
2 onions, finely chopped
2 celery stalks, finely chopped
3 garlic cloves, finely chopped
2 sprigs fresh thyme, leaves stripped
1½ tablespoons tomato purée
250 ml/8 fl oz dry red wine
75 g/3 oz oil-packed sun-dried tomatoes, drained, finely chopped
250 g/8 oz canned chopped Italian tomatoes in juice
Coarse salt
Freshly ground black pepper
6 tablespoons freshly grated Parmesan cheese

1 Make the polenta according to package directions, except use the stock and milk in place of the water called for. The mixture should be very thick. Rinse a 30 x 23-cm/12 x 9-inch roasting tray with water and shake it dry. Line the tray with baking parchment paper, and then mound the polenta on top. Dip a spatula in water and spread the polenta in an even layer, about 1 cm/½ inch thick. Allow to stand at room temperature for 1 hour.

2 Place a frying pan (with a lid) on the stovetop over a medium heat. Add 1 tablespoon oil and the sausage and cook for 6–8 minutes, until slightly browned and rendering some fat, stirring and breaking up the sausage with a wooden spoon. Add the onion and celery, cover, and reduce the heat to low. Cook for about 10 minutes, until the onion is slightly softened, stirring occasionally. Stir in the garlic and thyme and cook for 1 minute more. Stir in the tomato purée and wine, raise the heat, and deglaze the pan thoroughly; bring to a simmer and cook for 2–3 minutes, until reduced by about one-third. Add the sun-dried tomatoes, chopped tomatoes, ¼ teaspoon salt and ½ teaspoon pepper. Cover the pan, reduce the heat to very low, and simmer for 8–10 minutes, until thickened, stirring occasionally (check midway through, and add one or two tablespoons of water if necessary). Keep warm, covered.

3 Prepare the grill for direct cooking over high heat (230–290°C/450–550°F).

4 Cut the polenta into 12 rectangles, generously brush both sides with oil, season evenly with salt and pepper, and then grill over **grilling/direct high heat** for 6–8 minutes, with the lid closed, until nicely marked by the grill, turning once. Transfer to serving plates and immediately top with cheese and ragu.

SERVES: 4–6

LAMB KOFTA

WITH ROASTED RED PEPPER DIPPING SAUCE

PREP TIME: 40 minutes
CHILLING TIME: 1–2 hours
GRILLING TIME: 20–25 minutes
SPECIAL EQUIPMENT: 24 bamboo skewers, soaked in water for at
    least 30 minutes

KOFTA

1 kg/2 lb minced lamb
1 onion, finely chopped
4 tablespoons mint leaves, finely chopped
4 tablespoons fresh coriander leaves, finely chopped
2 teaspoons ground cumin
1½ teaspoons coarse salt
3 garlic cloves, finely chopped
1 teaspoon paprika
1 teaspoon ground coriander
½ teaspoon freshly ground black pepper
⅛ teaspoon ground cayenne pepper, or to taste

SAUCE

2 red peppers, each about 200 g/7 oz
1 red jalapeño chilli
1 tablespoon extra-virgin olive oil
1 teaspoon ground cumin
½ teaspoon coarse salt
½ teaspoon ground coriander
2 small garlic cloves, chopped
¼ teaspoon freshly ground black pepper
Extra-virgin olive oil

1 Mix the kofta ingredients, and then portion the mixture into 24 equal mounds. Gently form each mound around a skewer into a sausage 5–6 cm/2–2½ inches long by about 2.5 cm/1 inch wide. Place on a large baking sheet, cover with clingfilm, and refrigerate for 1–2 hours.

2 Prepare the grill for direct cooking over medium heat (180–230°C/350–450°F).

3 Grill the peppers and chilli over **grilling/indirect medium heat** for 10–12 minutes, with the lid closed, until blackened and blistered all over, turning occasionally. Place in a bowl and cover with clingfilm to trap the steam. Allow to stand for about 10 minutes. Remove and discard the charred skin, stalks, and seeds, and then roughly chops.

4 Place the chopped peppers and the remaining sauce ingredients in a food processor. Process until the mixture is smooth. Transfer to a bowl.

5 Lightly brush the kofta with oil. Working in batches, if necessary, grill the kofta over **grilling/direct medium heat** for about 10 minutes, with the lid closed, until cooked through and browned on all sides, turning as needed. Serve warm with the sauce.

SERVES: 6; 12 as an appetiser

CHICKEN SKEWERS

MARINATED IN BASIL AND SUN-DRIED TOMATOES

PREP TIME: 15 minutes
MARINATING TIME: 2–3 hours
GRILLING TIME: 6–8 minutes
SPECIAL EQUIPMENT: 8–12 metal or bamboo skewers (if using bamboo, soak in water for at least 30 minutes)

PASTE

25 g/1 oz fresh basil leaves
4 tablespoons oil-packed sun-dried tomatoes
3 garlic cloves
1 teaspoon sea salt
½ teaspoon ground black pepper
½ teaspoon dried oregano
6 tablespoons extra-virgin olive oil
2 tablespoons red wine vinegar

4 boneless, skinless chicken breasts, about 175 g/6 oz each

1 In the bowl of a food processor fitted with a metal blade, process the basil, tomatoes, garlic, salt, pepper and oregano until the tomatoes are finely chopped. Add the oil and vinegar and process to create a spreadable paste.

2 Cut each chicken breast in half lengthways and then cut each half crossways into 2.5–3.5 cm/1–1½-inch pieces. Place the chicken pieces in a large glass or stainless steel bowl and add the paste. Turn to coat the chicken pieces evenly. Cover and refrigerate for 2–3 hours.

3 Prepare the grill for direct cooking over high heat (230–290°C/450–550°F).

4 Thread the chicken pieces on to skewers, being sure to keep each skewer well within the flesh of the chicken. Discard any remaining paste.

5 Brush the cooking grates clean. Grill the skewers over **grilling/direct high heat** for 6–8 minutes, with the lid closed as much as possible, until the meat is firm to the touch and opaque all the way to the centre, turning once or twice. Remove from the grill and serve warm.

SERVES: 4

SALADS

NIÇOISE SALAD

WITH GRILLED TUNA AND CROÛTES

PREP TIME: 40 minutes
GRILLING TIME: 2–3 minutes

VINAIGRETTE

1 large shallot, finely chopped
1½ tablespoons red wine vinegar
2 teaspoons finely chopped flat-leaf parsley
1½ teaspoons Dijon mustard
1 garlic clove, finely chopped

Coarse salt
Freshly ground black pepper
Extra-virgin olive oil
8 golf ball-sized new potatoes, about 500 g/1 lb total, each cut
    into quarters
125 g/4 oz haricots verts or French beans, trimmed
2 tuna steaks, each 175–200 g/6–7 oz
4 slices rustic French or Italian bread, each about 1 cm/½ inch
    thick
1 garlic clove, peeled and cut in half
1 large head round lettuce
4–6 anchovy fillets, gently rinsed and patted dry
1 tablespoon capers, rinsed and drained
4 large hard-boiled eggs, each cut in half
50 g/2 oz niçoise olives or other brine-cured black olives

1 In a small bowl whisk the vinaigrette ingredients, including ½ teaspoon salt and ½ teaspoon pepper. Slowly add 75 ml/3 fl oz oil, whisking constantly to emulsify the vinaigrette. Set aside.

2 Bring a saucepan of salted water to the boil. Add the potatoes and boil for 7–10 minutes until tender when pierced with a knife but still holding their shape. Using a slotted spoon, transfer the potatoes to a colander and run cold water over them to stop the cooking. Drain and transfer to a bowl. Immediately add 2 tablespoons of the vinaigrette and toss to coat. Return the potato cooking water to the boil, if necessary. Add the beans and cook until crisp-tender and still bright green, 2–3 minutes for haricots verts and 4–5 minutes for larger green beans. Drain and refresh under cold running water, then cool and dry on kitchen paper.

3 Prepare the grill for direct cooking over high heat (230–290°C/450–550°F).

4 Lightly brush both sides of the tuna steaks with oil and season evenly with ½ teaspoon salt and ¼ teaspoon pepper. Brush the bread slices on each side with oil. Grill the tuna over **grilling/direct high heat**, with the lid open, until cooked to your desired doneness, 2–3 minutes for rare, turning once. During the last minute of grilling time, toast the bread over direct heat, turning once. Remove from the grill and rub one side of each bread slice with the cut side of the garlic.

5 Lay four lettuce leaves on each of four serving plates, and then arrange an equal amount of tuna, potatoes, beans, anchovies, capers, eggs, and olives evenly over the lettuce. Drizzle with the remaining vinaigrette. Serve with a croûte.

SERVES: 4

GRILLED CHICKEN SALAD NIÇOISE

WITH SHERRY VINAIGRETTE

PREP TIME: 35 minutes
GRILLING TIME: 8–12 minutes

VINAIGRETTE

175 ml/6 fl oz extra-virgin olive oil
4 tablespoons sherry vinegar
2 tablespoons finely chopped shallot
1½ tablespoons finely chopped marjoram
1 tablespoon Dijon mustard
½ teaspoon sea salt
¼ teaspoon ground black pepper

SALAD

6 small new potatoes, about 300 g/10 oz total
Sea salt
175 g/6 oz haricots verts (French beans), stems removed
4 boneless, skinless chicken breasts, about 175 g/6 oz each
1 small round lettuce, leaves separated
12 niçoise olives
3 plum tomatoes, cut crossways into 5-mm/¼-inch-thick slices
4 hard-boiled eggs, quartered

1 In a small glass or stainless-steel bowl, whisk the vinaigrette ingredients.

2 Prepare the grill for direct cooking over medium heat (180–230°C/350–450°F).

3 Fill a large saucepan three-quarters full with water and bring to the boil. Add the potatoes and boil for about 10 minutes, until barely tender. Remove the potatoes with a slotted spoon and, when cool enough to handle, cut them in half. Return the water to the boil, add a teaspoon or two of salt, and then add the green beans. Boil for 2–3 minutes until just crisp-tender. Drain and cool under cold running water.

4 Place the potatoes and chicken breasts in a shallow glass dish. Pour 4 tablespoons of the vinaigrette over them and turn to coat well. Reserve the remaining vinaigrette to dress the salad.

5 Brush the cooking grates clean. Grill the potatoes and the chicken, smooth (skin) side down first, over **grilling/ direct medium heat** for 8–12 minutes, with the lid closed as much as possible, until the potatoes are golden brown and the meat is firm to the touch and opaque all the way to the centre, turning once or twice. Remove from the grill and allow to rest for 3–5 minutes. Cut the chicken crossways into 5-mm/¼-inch slices.

6 Arrange a few lettuce leaves on each plate with some olives and tomatoes. Place the eggs, green beans and potatoes around the plate. Top with chicken slices. Drizzle the reserved vinaigrette over the salad. Serve at room temperature.

SERVES: 4

PICNIC CHICKEN PROVENÇAL

WITH WHITE BEAN SALAD

PREP TIME: 30 minutes
MARINATING TIME: 2–4 hours
GRILLING TIME: 30–50 minutes

MARINADE

1 small onion, roughly chopped
25 g/1 oz flat-leaf parsley leaves and tender stems
4 tablespoons fresh rosemary leaves
4 large garlic cloves
2 tablespoons Dijon mustard
2 tablespoons tomato purée
2 teaspoons sea salt
1/2 teaspoon ground black pepper
125 ml/4 fl oz dry white wine
4 tablespoons extra-virgin olive oil

1 whole chicken, 2–2.5 kg/4–5 lb

DRESSING

4 tablespoons extra-virgin olive oil
2 tablespoons red wine vinegar
1 teaspoon finely chopped garlic
1/2 teaspoon sea salt
1/4 teaspoon ground black pepper

SALAD

2 cans (410 g/13 oz each) cannellini beans, rinsed
200 g/7 oz cherry tomatoes, finely chopped
75 g/3 oz green olives, sliced
5 tablespoons flat-leaf parsley, roughly chopped

1 In a food processor or blender, process the marinade ingredients, except the wine and oil, until finely chopped. Then add the wine and oil and process until fairly smooth. Pour the marinade into a large glass or stainless-steel bowl.

2 Cut the chicken into eight pieces: two breast pieces, two thigh pieces, two drumsticks and two wings. Add the chicken pieces to the bowl with the marinade and turn to coat evenly. Cover and refrigerate for 2–4 hours.

3 In a large bowl whisk the dressing ingredients. Add the salad ingredients and stir gently to combine. Set aside at room temperature until ready to serve.

4 Prepare the grill for direct and indirect cooking over medium heat (180–230°C/350–450°F).

5 Remove the chicken pieces from the bowl and discard the marinade. Brush the cooking grates clean. Grill the chicken, skin side down first, over **roasting/indirect medium heat**, with the lid closed, until the juices run clear and the meat is opaque all the way to the bone, turning two or three times. The breasts and wings will take 30–40 minutes and the thighs and drumsticks will take 40–50 minutes. During the last 10 minutes of grilling time, move the chicken over **grilling/direct medium heat** until well browned all over, turning once. Remove from the grill and allow to rest for 3–5 minutes.

6 Place the salad in a wide, shallow bowl and arrange the chicken pieces on top.

SERVES: 4–6

GRILLED BREAD SALAD

WITH CHICKEN, CURRANTS AND PINE NUTS

PREP TIME: 25 minutes
GRILLING TIME: 10–15 minutes
SPECIAL EQUIPMENT: perforated grill pan

VINAIGRETTE

1 large garlic clove, finely chopped
1½ tablespoons balsamic vinegar
1 tablespoon mayonnaise
1 tablespoon Dijon mustard

Coarse salt
Freshly ground black pepper
Extra-virgin olive oil
4 boneless, skinless chicken breasts, each about 175 g/6 oz
15 g/½ oz unsalted butter, melted
175 g/6 oz slightly stale French or Italian bread, crust removed, cut into 2.5-cm/1-inch cubes
150 g/5 oz mixed salas leaves including radicchio
50 g/2 oz dried currants
40 g/1½ oz toasted pine nuts (see Note)
¼ small red onion or 1 large shallot, cut into thin slices

NOTE!

Pine nuts may be toasted in a 180°C/350°F/gas mark 4 oven for 5–7 minutes or in a dry frying pan over a medium heat; don't leave unattended, or they can quickly burn. Be sure to transfer nuts from the hot pan once they are cooked so they will not continue cooking.

1 In a large serving bowl combine the vinaigrette ingredients, including ½ teaspoon salt and ¼ teaspoon pepper. Slowly add 75 ml/3 fl oz oil, whisking constantly to emulsify the vinaigrette. Set aside.

2 Brush the chicken breasts on both sides with oil and season evenly with salt and pepper.

3 In a separate bowl whisk 3 tablespoons oil and the melted butter. Add the bread cubes and toss to coat.

4 Prepare the grill for direct cooking over medium-high heat (200–230°C/400–450°F) and preheat a perforated grill pan for about 10 minutes.

5 Spread the bread cubes in a single layer on the pan and grill over **grilling/direct medium-high heat** for 2–3 minutes, with the lid open, until golden brown, watching carefully and turning once or twice. Immediately transfer the cubes to the bowl with the dressing. Wearing insulated barbecue mitts or ovengloves, remove the grill pan from the grill.

6 Grill the chicken over **grilling/direct medium-high heat** for 8–12 minutes, with the lid closed, until the meat is firm to the touch and opaque all the way to the centre, turning once. Remove from the grill and cut into bite-sized pieces.

7 To the large serving bowl add the chicken, salad leaves, currants, pine nuts and onion and toss thoroughly. If liked, season with additional salt and pepper. Divide among four plates and serve right away.

SERVES: 4

TAGLIATA OF SKIRT STEAK

WITH ROCKET AND SHAVED PARMESAN

PREP TIME: 15 minutes
GRILLING TIME: 6–8 minutes

1 piece of skirt steak, 750 g–1 kg/1½–2 lb and about
    1.5 cm/¾ inch thick
Extra-virgin olive oil
Sea salt
Ground black pepper
75 ml/3 fl oz balsamic vinegar
½ teaspoon granulated sugar
250 g/8 oz baby rocket
100 g/3½ oz shaved Parmesan cheese

1 Lightly brush the steak on both sides with oil and season evenly with salt and pepper. Allow the steak to stand at room temperature for 15–30 minutes before grilling.

2 Prepare the grill for direct cooking over high heat (200–230°C/450–550°F).

3 In a small saucepan over a medium-high heat, combine the vinegar and sugar. Allow the mixture to reduce by half, 6–8 minutes, stirring occasionally. Remove from the heat and leave to cool.

4 Brush the cooking grates clean. Grill the steak over **grilling/direct high heat**, with the lid closed as much as possible, until cooked to your desired doneness, 6–8 minutes for medium rare, turning once or twice (if flare-ups occur, move the steak temporarily over indirect heat). Transfer to a chopping board and allow to rest for 3–5 minutes.

5 Cut the steak in half lengthways and then cut each half across the grain into thin slices; divide evenly on serving plates. Pour any juices remaining on the chopping board over the steak, and pile the rocket on top. Drizzle each serving of rocket with oil and the balsamic reduction, season with salt and pepper, and top with the cheese.

SERVES: 4–6

STEAK HOUSE SALAD

WITH BLUE CHEESE VINAIGRETTE

PREP TIME: 15 minutes
GRILLING TIME: 6–8 minutes

SALAD

3 romaine lettuce hearts, halved, cored and coarsely chopped
500 g/1 lb cherry tomatoes, halved
25 g/1 oz flat-leaf parsley
½ red onion, sliced into paper-thin half-moons

4 sirloin steaks, each 300–375 g/10–12 oz and about 2.5 cm/
    1 inch thick, trimmed of excess fat
Extra-virgin olive oil
Sea salt
Ground black pepper

VINAIGRETTE

125 ml/4 fl oz extra-virgin olive oil
40 g/1½ oz blue cheese, crumbled
4 tablespoons red wine vinegar
1 teaspoon sea salt
½ teaspoon ground black pepper

1 In a large bowl combine the salad ingredients.

2 Lightly brush the steaks on both sides with oil and season evenly with salt and pepper. Allow the steaks to stand at room temperature for 15–30 minutes before grilling.

3 Prepare the grill for direct cooking over high heat (200–230°C/450–550°F).

4 Brush the cooking grates clean. Grill the steaks over **grilling/direct high heat**, with the lid closed as much as possible, until cooked to your desired doneness, 6–8 minutes for medium rare, turning once or twice (if flare-ups occur, move the steaks temporarily over indirect heat). Transfer the steaks to a chopping board and allow to rest for 3–5 minutes.

5 While the steaks rest, whisk the vinaigrette ingredients in a small bowl. Drizzle the salad with the vinaigrette and toss to coat. Divide the salad evenly among individual serving plates.

6 Cut the steaks into thin slices. Pile steak on top of each salad and serve with any remaining dressing.

SERVES: 6–8

SKIRT STEAK GYROS

WITH FRESH CUCUMBER SALAD

PREP TIME: 45 minutes
MARINATING TIME: 2–4 hours
GRILLING TIME: 8–10 minutes

MARINADE

125 ml/4 fl oz extra-virgin olive oil
4 tablespoons fresh lemon juice
4 tablespoons roughly chopped oregano leaves
1 tablespoon finely chopped garlic
2 teaspoons coarsely ground black pepper
½ teaspoon sea salt
1 piece of skirt steak, 750 g–1 kg/1½–2 lb and about 1.5 cm/
    ¾ inch thick

SALAD

150 g/5 oz romaine lettuce, coarsely shredded
25 kalamata olives, pitted
150 g/5 oz cucumber, peeled and finely diced
200 g/7 oz ripe tomatoes, finely diced
½ small red onion, finely diced

SAUCE

250 g/8 oz Greek yogurt
3 tablespoons finely chopped mint
½ teaspoon sea salt
¼ teaspoon ground black pepper
4 pitta breads, cut in half

1 In a medium bowl whisk the marinade ingredients. Set aside 4 tablespoons of the marinade to dress the salad.

2 Put the steak in a 33 x 23-cm/13 x 9-inch glass dish and pour in the marinade. Turn to coat both sides. Cover and refrigerate for 2–4 hours, turning occasionally. Allow the steak to stand at room temperature for 15–30 minutes before grilling.

3 In a medium bowl combine the salad ingredients and set aside until ready to serve.

4 Prepare the grill for direct cooking over medium heat (180–230°C/350–450°F).

5 Brush the cooking grates clean. Remove the steak from the marinade, letting the excess liquid drip back into the dish. Discard the marinade. Grill the steak over **grilling/direct medium heat**, with the lid closed as much as possible, until cooked to your desired doneness, 8–10 minutes for medium rare, turning once or twice (if flare-ups occur, move the steak temporarily over indirect heat). Remove from the grill and allow to rest for 3–5 minutes.

6 Cut the steak in half lengthways and then across the grain into thin slices. Cut the slices into bite-sized pieces.

7 In a small bowl whisk the sauce ingredients.

8 Dress the salad with the reserved marinade and toss to coat. Fill each pitta half with steak, salad, and then top with a spoonful of sauce. Serve warm.

SERVES: 4–6

PENNE SALAD

WITH ITALIAN SAUSAGE, ROASTED TOMATOES AND SAGE

PREP TIME: 30 minutes
GRILLING TIME: 8–10 minutes
SPECIAL EQUIPMENT: perforated grill pan

4 firm, almost-ripe tomatoes, each about 175 g/6 oz
1 tablespoon extra-virgin olive oil
2 garlic cloves, finely chopped
2 teaspoons chopped sage
Coarse salt
Freshly ground black pepper
500 g/1 lb fresh Italian sausages, mild and/or spicy

VINAIGRETTE

2 large shallots, finely chopped
75 ml/3 fl oz extra-virgin olive oil
1 tablespoon Dijon mustard
1 tablespoon red wine vinegar

500 g/1 lb dried penne
50 g/2 oz baby rocket or baby spinach leaves, roughly chopped
50 g/2 oz pecorino cheese, grated using the large holes of a
    box grater

1 Prepare the grill for direct cooking over medium-high heat (200–260°C/400–500°F) and preheat a perforated grill pan for about 5 minutes.

2 Cut the tomatoes lengthways into quarters, core and seed them, and reserve the juices to use in the vinaigrette. Place the tomatoes on kitchen paper, cut side down, and allow to stand for 5 minutes.

3 In a medium bowl whisk the oil, garlic, sage, 1/2 teaspoon salt and 1/4 teaspoon pepper. Add the tomato quarters and turn to coat. Place the tomatoes on the grill pan, cut side down, and grill over **grilling/direct medium-high heat** for 3–4 minutes, with the lid closed, until marked by the grill but not soft or falling apart, turning once. At the same time, grill the sausages over **grilling/direct medium-high heat** for 8–10 minutes, until fully cooked (70°C/160°F), turning occasionally. Remove from the grill as they are done. When cool enough to handle, roughly chop the tomatoes and cut the sausages into 1-cm/1/2-inch diagonal slices, and then cut the slices in half.

4 In a large bowl whisk the vinaigrette ingredients, including the reserved tomato juices, 1 teaspoon salt and 1/2 teaspoon pepper.

5 Bring a large saucepan of water to the boil and add 1 tablespoon salt. Add the penne and cook according to package instructions, stirring frequently. Drain the pasta well and immediately add it to the bowl with the vinaigrette; toss to coat evenly. Fold in the tomatoes, sausage pieces, rocket, and all but a small handful of the cheese. Taste and adjust the seasoning with a generous amount of salt and pepper. Scatter the remaining handful of cheese over the top and serve warm, at room temperature or chilled.

SERVES: 4–6

COUSCOUS SALAD

WITH GRILLED LAMB, FETA AND MINT

PREP TIME: 20 minutes
GRILLING TIME: 4–6 minutes

625 g/1¼ lb boneless leg of lamb or boneless lamb steaks,
    cut into 1-cm/½-inch-thick slices
Extra-virgin olive oil
Coarse salt
Freshly ground black pepper
½ teaspoon dried thyme
325 g/11 oz onion, finely chopped
250 g/8 oz Israeli giant couscous
500 ml/17 fl oz chicken stock
Finely grated zest and juice of 1 lemon
5 tablespoons finely chopped mint
125 g/4 oz feta cheese, finely crumbled

1 Brush the lamb slices on both sides with 2 tablespoons oil and season with ¾ teaspoon salt, ½ teaspoon pepper and the thyme. Allow to stand for up to an hour at room temperature or 2 hours, refrigerated. If chilled, leave at room temperature for 15–30 minutes before grilling.

2 Prepare the grill for direct cooking over medium-high heat (200–230°C/400–450°F).

3 In a saucepan over a medium heat, warm 1 tablespoon oil. Add the onion and sauté for about 5 minutes, until slightly softened, stirring occasionally. Add the couscous and continue cooking and stirring for 5–6 minutes until the couscous is just beginning to brown. Add the chicken stock, 1 teaspoon salt and ¼ teaspoon pepper. Bring to the boil over a high heat, reduce the heat to medium-low, partially cover the pan and simmer for 8–10 minutes, until the couscous is tender and all the liquid is absorbed. Transfer to a large bowl and add 4 tablespoons olive oil. Fluff with a fork.

4 Grill the lamb over **grilling/direct medium-high heat**, with the lid closed, until cooked to your desired doneness, 4–6 minutes for medium rare, turning once. Remove from the grill and allow to rest for 5 minutes.

5 Fold the lemon zest and juice, about three-quarters of the mint and the feta into the couscous. Taste for seasoning and fluff again. Divide the couscous among four plates. Cut the lamb slices crossways into bite-sized pieces and arrange on top of the couscous. Garnish with the remaining mint.

SERVES: 4

NOTE!

Giant couscous is also called Israeli or pearl couscous. The dish works equally well with orzo pasta.

GREEN BEAN AND MUSHROOM SALAD

WITH GRILLED HALLOUMI CHEESE

PREP TIME: 20 minutes
GRILLING TIME: 4–6 minutes
SPECIAL EQUIPMENT: perforated grill pan

500 g/1 lb haricots verts or thin French beans, trimmed
175 g/6 oz halloumi cheese, cut into 1-cm/½-inch-thick
    rectangles
Extra-virgin olive oil spray
Freshly ground black pepper
75 ml/3 fl oz extra-virgin olive oil
2 tablespoons fresh lemon juice
2 tablespoons pine nuts, toasted and roughly chopped
½ teaspoon coarse salt
175 g/6 oz button or chestnut mushrooms, wiped clean and
    cut into 5-mm/¼-inch slices

1 In a large saucepan of salted, boiling water blanch the green beans for 2–4 minutes, depending on their size (they should be bright green and still slightly crunchy). Immediately drain in a colander, and then run cold water over the beans until cool. Spread on a roasting tray lined with kitchen paper for up to 2 hours before serving. If the beans are longer than 7 cm/ 3 inches, cut them crossways in half.

2 Prepare the grill for direct cooking over medium-high heat (200–230°C/400–450°F) and preheat a perforated grill pan.

3 Spray the cheese lightly on both sides with oil and season with a pinch of pepper. Grill the cheese over **grilling/direct medium-high heat** for 4–6 minutes, with the lid open, until golden brown but not melted, turning once with a metal spatula. Remove from the grill and allow to rest for 5 minutes. Cut the cheese rectangles lengthways into thirds, and then crossways into 1-cm/½-inch cubes (don't worry if they fall apart).

4 In a medium, shallow serving bowl whisk the oil, lemon juice, pine nuts, salt and ½ teaspoon pepper. Add the green beans and mushrooms; toss to combine thoroughly. Scatter the halloumi cheese cubes on top and serve.

SERVES: 4

ROCKET SALAD

WITH GRILLED PEARS, PECORINO AND HAZELNUTS

PREP TIME: 10 minutes
GRILLING TIME: 6–8 minutes

4 tablespoons hazelnuts

DRESSING
1 small shallot, finely chopped
2 tablespoons red wine vinegar
1 tablespoon fresh lemon juice
1 teaspoon Dijon mustard
½ teaspoon coarse salt
¼ teaspoon freshly ground black pepper

75 ml/3 fl oz extra-virgin olive oil
2 firm but ripe pears, cut lengthways in half and cored (do not peel)
250 g/8 oz baby rocket
25 g/1 oz pecorino cheese, shaved with a vegetable peeler

1 Preheat the oven to 180°C/350°F/gas mark 4. Spread the hazelnuts in a single layer on a small, rimmed baking tray. Bake for 10–12 minutes, until fragrant and toasted, shaking the tray once or twice. Allow to cool. To remove the skin, rub together between your palms or in kitchen paper. Coarsely chop and set aside.

2 In a small bowl whisk the dressing ingredients. Then slowly add the olive oil, whisking constantly to emulsify the dressing.

3 Prepare the grill for direct cooking over medium heat (180–230°C/350–450°F).

4 Lightly brush the pear halves all over with some of the dressing. Grill the pears, cut side down, over **grilling/ direct medium heat** for 4–5 minutes, with the lid closed, until lightly charred and starting to soften. Turn the pears over and brush with a little of the dressing. Continue to grill for 2–3 minutes more, until the pears are tender but still firm. Remove from the grill and cool for 5 minutes. Starting from 2.5 cm/1 inch below the top of the pear, cut each pear lengthways into 5-mm/¼-inch slices, while maintaining the pear shape.

5 In a large bowl combine the rocket, cheese, and enough of the remaining dressing to lightly coat the rocket. Mix well. Divide the salad among six serving plates. Fan several slices of pear over the rocket. Garnish with the hazelnuts. Serve right away.

SERVES: 6

FISH AND SHELLFISH

TUNA STEAKS

WITH MINTY CUCUMBER AND RAISIN SALSA

PREP TIME: 15 minutes
GRILLING TIME: 5–6 minutes

SALSA
200 g/7 oz peeled, seeded and diced cucumber
4 tablespoons chopped sultanas
4 tablespoons finely chopped mint
2 tablespoons finely chopped red onion
2 tablespoons olive oil
1 tablespoon fresh lemon juice
1½ teaspoons capers, rinsed and chopped
¼ teaspoon freshly ground black pepper
¼ teaspoon coarse salt

PASTE
4 tablespoons olive oil
1 tablespoon chopped dill
1 tablespoon chopped oregano leaves
1 tablespoon finely chopped garlic
1 teaspoon finely grated lemon zest
1 teaspoon coarse salt
½ teaspoon crushed chilli flakes

4 tuna steaks, each about 175 g/6 oz and 1.5 cm/¾ inch thick

1 Combine the salsa ingredients. Set the salsa aside until ready to serve.

2 Mix the paste ingredients. Spread and massage the paste over the tuna steaks to coat evenly.

3 Prepare the grill for direct cooking over high heat (230–290°C/450–550°F).

4 Grill the tuna over **grilling/direct high heat**, with the lid closed, until cooked to your desired doneness, 5–6 minutes for medium, turning once. Remove from the grill and serve warm with the salsa.

SERVES: 4

SALMON

WITH GREEN OLIVE TAPENADE

PREP TIME: 20 minutes
GRILLING TIME: 6–10 minutes

TAPENADE

4 tablespoons almonds with skin, toasted
275 g/9 oz pitted green olives, such as picholine
3 tablespoons extra-virgin olive oil
2 tablespoons finely chopped flat-leaf parsley (optional)
2 teaspoons capers, rinsed
1 teaspoon finely grated lemon zest
1 teaspoon fresh lemon juice
½ teaspoon freshly ground black pepper
1 garlic clove, chopped

6 salmon fillets (with skin), each 175–250 g/6–8 oz and about
    2.5 cm/1 inch thick, pin bones removed
Extra-virgin olive oil
1 teaspoon coarse salt
¾ teaspoon freshly ground black pepper
1 lemon, cut into 6 wedges

1 Place the almonds in a food processor. Pulse until coarsely chopped. Add the remaining tapenade ingredients and pulse until finely chopped.

2 Prepare the grill for direct cooking over high heat (230–290°C/450–550°F).

3 Generously brush the flesh side of the salmon fillets with oil and season evenly with the salt and pepper. Grill the fillets, flesh side down first, over **grilling/direct high heat** for 4–6 minutes, with the lid closed, until you can lift them off the cooking grates without sticking. Turn the fillets over and continue cooking to your desired doneness, 2–4 minutes more for medium rare. If desired, remove the skin by slipping a spatula between the skin and flesh and transfer the fillets to serving plates. Top each fillet with 2–3 tablespoons of the tapenade (reserve any remaining tapenade for another use). Serve with lemon wedges.

SERVES: 6

NOTE!

Do not overprocess the tapenade or it will become a paste. The tapenade may be made up to 2 days in advance of serving.

SWORDFISH

WITH TOMATO, RED PEPPER, OLIVE AND WHITE WINE SAUCE

PREP TIME: 30 minutes
GRILLING TIME: 15–19 minutes

1 bell pepper, 200–250 g/7–8 oz
Extra-virgin olive oil
1 large garlic clove, finely chopped
¼ teaspoon crushed chilli flakes
1 can (400 g/13 oz) whole Italian plum tomatoes in juice
125 ml/4 fl oz cup dry white wine
½ teaspoon dried oregano
75 g/3 oz pitted Kalamata olives, drained, halved lengthways
1½ tablespoons red wine vinegar
Coarse salt
Freshly ground black pepper
4 swordfish steaks, each 175–250 g/6–8 oz and about
    2.5 cm/1 inch thick
4 tablespoons finely chopped flat-leaf parsley

1 Prepare the grill for direct cooking over high heat
(230–290°C/450–550°F).

2 Grill the pepper over **grilling/direct high heat** for 10–12 minutes, with the lid closed, until blackened and blistered all over, turning occasionally. Place the pepper in a bowl and cover with clingfilm to trap the steam. Allow to stand for about 10 minutes. Remove and discard the charred skin, stalk, and seeds, and cut the pepper into 5-mm/¼-inch strips.

3 In a frying pan over a medium heat, warm 1 tablespoon oil. Add the garlic and crushed chilli and sauté for about 1 minute, until fragrant. Add the tomatoes, wine and oregano. Bring to the boil, and then reduce the heat to medium-low. Simmer for 5 minutes. Add the pepper strips, olives, vinegar, ¾ teaspoon salt and ¼ teaspoon pepper. Cook, uncovered, over a medium-low heat for 10–12 minutes, until the sauce is slightly thickened, stirring occasionally and breaking up the tomatoes with a spoon.

4 Brush the swordfish steaks generously with oil, season evenly with ¾ teaspoon salt and ½ teaspoon pepper, and then grill over **grilling/direct high heat** for 5–7 minutes, with the lid closed, until just opaque in the centre but still juicy, turning once. Transfer to serving plates. Spoon some of the sauce over the steaks. Garnish with parsley and serve immediately.

SERVES: 4

NOTE!

Other firm white fish, such as halibut or monkfish, may be substituted for the swordfish. Adjust the grilling time accordingly, depending on thickness.

SEA BASS

WITH ORANGE, FENNEL AND PARSLEY GREMOLATA

PREP TIME: 10 minutes
MARINATING TIME: up to 30 minutes
GRILLING TIME: 8–10 minutes

MARINADE

2 tablespoons fresh orange juice
2 tablespoons extra-virgin olive oil
½ teaspoon coarse salt
¼ teaspoon freshly ground black pepper

4 sea bass fillets, each 175–250 g/6–8 oz and 2.5–3.5 cm/
    1–1½ inches thick

GREMOLATA

15 g/½ oz flat-leaf parsley, finely chopped
15 g/½ fennel fronds and sprigs, finely chopped
2 tablespoons finely chopped unsalted pistachio nuts
2 tablespoons extra-virgin olive oil
1 teaspoon finely grated orange zest
2 teaspoons fresh orange juice
¼ teaspoon coarse salt
⅛ teaspoon freshly ground black pepper

1 In a small bowl whisk the marinade ingredients.

2 Arrange the fillets in a shallow, rimmed baking dish, and pour in the marinade; turn the fillets to coat. Cover and refrigerate while you make the gremolata. Do not marinate longer than 30 minutes.

3 Prepare the grill for direct cooking over high heat (230–290°C/450–550°F).

4 In a medium bowl mix the gremolata ingredients.

5 Grill the fillets over **grilling/direct high heat** for 4–5 minutes, with the lid closed, until you can lift the fillets off the cooking grates without sticking. Turn the fillets over and continue cooking until just cooked through, 4–5 minutes more. Spoon the gremolata over the fillets and serve immediately.

SERVES: 4

MONKFISH

WITH BASIL AND PARSLEY PESTO

PREP TIME: 20 minutes
GRILLING TIME: 7–9 minutes

2 small garlic cloves
25 g/1 oz basil leaves
4 tablespoons flat-leaf parsley
50 g/2 oz freshly grated Parmesan cheese
1 tablespoon toasted pine nuts
Coarse salt
Extra-virgin olive oil
750 g/1½ lb monkfish, any blue-grey membrane trimmed,
    cut into roughly 2.5-cm/1-inch medallions
¼ teaspoon freshly ground black pepper

1 Place the garlic in a small food processor and process until very finely chopped, stopping to scrape the inside of the bowl as needed. Add the basil, parsley, cheese, pine nuts and ½ teaspoon salt and blend until smooth, stopping to scrape the inside of the bowl as needed. With the machine running, slowly drizzle in 75 ml/3 fl oz oil and process until blended completely. Transfer to a small bowl, cover, and allow to stand for at least 30 minutes.

2 Prepare the grill for direct cooking over high heat (230–290°C/450–550°F).

3 Brush the monkfish medallions on both sides with oil, season evenly with ¾ teaspoon salt and the pepper, and then grill over **grilling/direct high heat** for about 4 minutes, with the lid closed, until you can lift them off the cooking grates without sticking. Turn them over and continue cooking until the flesh is opaque in the centre but still moist, 3–5 minutes more. Serve the medallions warm with a generous dollop of pesto on top.

SERVES: 4

NOTE!

If monkfish is not available, substitute four firm-fleshed white fish fillets, such as cod or halibut, each fillet about 200 g/7 oz and 1.5–2.5cm/¾–1 inch thick.

GRILLED SEA BASS

WITH HAZELNUT BROWN BUTTER

PREP TIME: 20 minutes
GRILLING TIME: 6–10 minutes
SPECIAL EQUIPMENT: perforated grill pan

2 whole sea bass, each 375–500 g/12–16 oz, cleaned, scaled and rinsed (keep refrigerated until ready to use)
Extra-virgin olive oil
1 teaspoon coarse salt
½ teaspoon freshly ground black pepper
1 lemon, cut into half-moons
4 garlic cloves, thinly sliced
4 sprigs fresh thyme
4 sprigs flat-leaf parsley
50 g/2 oz unsalted butter
3 tablespoons coarsely chopped hazelnuts
2 tablespoons finely chopped assorted herbs, such as dill, parsley, basil and/or chives

1 Prepare the grill for direct cooking over high heat (230–290°C/450–550°F) and preheat a perforated grill pan.

2 Lightly coat the outside of the fish with oil and season the inside and outside of each with ½ teaspoon salt and ¼ teaspoon pepper. Stuff the cavity of each fish with an equal amount of the sliced lemons, garlic and thyme and parsley sprigs. Transfer the fish to the grill pan and grill over **grilling/direct high heat**, with the lid closed, for 3–5 minutes (depending on the thickness) without moving. Release with a metal spatula, turn, and continue grilling until nicely charred on both sides and the flesh near the bone is opaque but still juicy, 3–5 minutes more. Transfer to a large serving plate.

3 In a small saucepan over a medium heat, melt the butter with the hazelnuts for 3–5 minutes, swirling the mixture until it just begins to turn nut-brown. Remove from the heat and pour over the fish. Garnish with the chopped herbs. Serve immediately.

SERVES: 2

CATALAN FISH STEW

WITH GRILLED CHORIZO AND FENNEL

PREP TIME: 35 minutes
GRILLING TIME: 30–33 minutes
SPECIAL EQUIPMENT: grill-proof cast-iron casserole

375 g/12 oz Spanish chorizo sausage, cut on the diagonal into 1-cm/½-inch slices
1 tablespoon extra-virgin olive oil, if needed
1 fennel bulb, about 375 g/12 oz, cored and thinly sliced
2 onions, finely chopped
4 garlic cloves, finely chopped
125 ml/4 fl oz dry white wine
2 tablespoons tomato purée
1 teaspoon paprika
½ teaspoon saffron threads
⅛ teaspoon ground cayenne pepper, or to taste
750 ml/1¼ pints chicken stock
2 cans (each 400 g/13 oz) chopped Italian plum tomatoes in juice
1 bay leaf
1 teaspoon coarse salt
1 teaspoon granulated sugar
½ teaspoon freshly ground black pepper
750 g/1½ lb sea bass or halibut fillets, about 3.5 cm/1½ inches thick, cut into 3.5 cm/1½-inch chunks
18 raw king prawns, peeled and deveined, tails removed
18 live mussels, about 375 g/12 oz total, scrubbed and debearded
4 tablespoons chopped flat-leaf parsley

1 Prepare the grill for direct and indirect cooking over medium heat (180–230°C/350–450°F) and preheat a cast-iron casserole, without its lid, over direct heat.

2 Put the chorizo in the casserole and grill over **grilling/ direct medium heat** for about 3 minutes, with the lid closed, until golden brown on both sides, turning once or twice. Using a slotted spoon, transfer the chorizo to a plate.

3 There should be rendered fat from the chorizo remaining in the casserole. If not, add 1 tablespoon oil. Add the fennel and onion and sauté for 6–7 minutes, with the lid closed, until slightly softened. Add the garlic and sauté until fragrant, about 1 minute. Add the wine and cook for another minute, with the lid open, until reduced by half, stirring occasionally. Add the tomato purée, paprika, saffron and cayenne. Stir for about 1 minute, until fragrant and blended. Add the chicken stock, tomatoes, bay leaf, salt, sugar and black pepper. Simmer over **grilling/direct medium heat**, partially covered with the casserole lid and with the grill lid closed, for 15 minutes.

4 Stir in the chorizo and any accumulated juices. Add the fish and submerge in the stock, and then stir in the prawns and mussels. Partially cover the casserole and cook over **grilling/direct medium heat** for 3–5 minutes, with the grill lid closed, until the fish and prawns are just opaque in the centre and the mussels open. Discard the bay leaf and any unopened mussels.

5 Ladle the stew into bowls. Garnish with the parsley and serve immediately.

SERVES: 6

STEAMED MUSSELS IN ANISE LIQUEUR

WITH TOMATOES AND FENNEL

PREP TIME: 10 minutes
GRILLING TIME: 25 minutes
SPECIAL EQUIPMENT: grill-proof cast-iron casserole

1 French baguette, about 425 g/14 oz, cut on the diagonal into 2.5-cm/1-inch slices
Extra-virgin olive oil
1 small onion, finely chopped
1 fennel bulb, about 300 g/10 oz, fronds trimmed, bulb cut lengthways in half, cored, and thinly sliced
3 garlic cloves, finely chopped
1 can (400 g/13 oz) whole Italian plum tomatoes in juice, drained and coarsely chopped
350 ml/12 fl oz dry white wine
4 tablespoons anise liqueur
1 teaspoon finely chopped thyme leaves
1½ teaspoons coarse salt
½ teaspoon freshly ground black pepper
1 kg/2 lb live mussels, scrubbed and debearded
2 tablespoons roughly chopped flat-leaf parsley

1 Prepare the grill for direct cooking over medium heat (180–230°C/350–450°F).

2 Brush the bread slices on both sides with oil.

3 In a grill-proof cast-iron casserole set over **grilling/direct medium heat,** warm 1 tablespoon oil. Add the onion and fennel and cook for 4–5 minutes, with the lid closed, until softened, stirring frequently. Add the garlic and cook for about 1 minute, until fragrant, stirring frequently. Add the tomatoes, white wine, anise liqueur, thyme, salt and pepper. Bring to the boil over **grilling/direct medium heat,** with the grill lid closed, and then simmer for 2 minutes. Stir in the mussels, cover the casserole with its lid, and cook over **grilling/direct medium heat** for 4–6 minutes, with the grill lid closed, until the mussels open. Discard any unopened mussels. During the last minute of grilling time, toast the baguette slices over direct heat, turning once.

4 Ladle the mussels and broth into serving bowls. Garnish with the parsley and serve immediately with the baguette slices.

SERVES: 4

PANCETTA-WRAPPED TIGER PRAWNS

PREP TIME: 30 minutes
MARINATING TIME: at least 2 hours or up to 4 hours
GRILLING TIME: 5–7 minutes
SPECIAL EQUIPMENT: cocktail sticks, perforated grill pan

MARINADE/VINAIGRETTE
2 small roasted red peppers (from a jar), coarsely chopped
6 tablespoons extra-virgin olive oil
6 large, fresh basil leaves
2 tablespoons red wine vinegar
1¼ teaspoons balsamic vinegar
½ teaspoon smoked paprika
½ teaspoon coarse salt
1 garlic clove, finely chopped
¼ teaspoon freshly ground black pepper

18 tiger prawns, peeled, deveined and butterflied, tails left on
9 slices pancetta or Parma ham, each cut in half
175 g/6 oz baby salad leaves

1 In a blender or food processor combine the marinade/vinaigrette ingredients and pulse until smooth. In a bowl combine half the marinade with the prawns and toss gently to coat them evenly. Cover and refrigerate for at least 2 hours or, preferably, up to 4 hours. Refrigerate the remaining vinaigrette.

2 Prepare the grill for direct cooking over medium-high heat (200–260°C/400–500°F) and preheat a perforated grill pan.

3 Using a slotted spoon, lift the prawns from the bowl; discard the marinade. Wrap each prawn with a half slice of pancetta, wrapping it around in a spiral. Insert a cocktail stick diagonally through the prawn to secure the pancetta. Grill the wrapped prawns on the grill pan over **grilling/direct medium-high heat** for 3 minutes, with the lid closed. Turn and continue grilling until the pancetta is crisp and the prawns are firm to the touch and just turning opaque in the centre. Remove from the grill.

4 Lightly coat the salad leaves with some of the remaining vinaigrette; spread the leaves on a serving plate. Remove the cocktail sticks from the prawns. Place the prawns on the leaves and serve right away.

SERVES: 4

INSALATA DI FRUTTI DI MARE

PREP TIME: 15 minutes
GRILLING TIME: 7–12 minutes
SPECIAL EQUIPMENT: perforated grill pan

DRESSING
1 teaspoon finely grated lemon zest
3 tablespoons fresh lemon juice
2 garlic cloves, finely chopped
1 teaspoon runny honey

Extra-virgin olive oil
Coarse salt
Freshly ground black pepper
12 large scallops, each about 40 g/1½ oz, patted dry
12 extra-large raw prawns, peeled and deveined
375 g/12 oz cleaned baby squid, tubes and tentacles separated, defrosted if frozen
1 red jalapeño chilli, thinly sliced
4 tablespoons chopped flat-leaf parsley
125 g/4 oz mixed salad leaves with rocket
Lemon wedges

1 Whisk the dressing ingredients, including 75 ml/3 fl oz oil, ½ teaspoon salt and ½ teaspoon pepper.

2 Prepare the grill for direct cooking over high heat (230–290°C/450–550°F) and preheat a perforated grill pan for 10 minutes.

3 Remove and discard the small, tough side muscle that might be left on each scallop. In a large bowl mix 3 tablespoons oil, 1 teaspoon salt, and ½ teaspoon pepper. Add the scallops, prawns and squid and turn to coat.

4 Grill the scallops, prawns and squid on the grill pan over **grilling/direct high heat**, with the lid closed, until the scallops are lightly browned and just opaque in the centre, 3–5 minutes; the prawns are just firm to the touch and opaque in the centre, 2–4 minutes; and the squid is beginning to turn golden on both sides, 2–3 minutes, turning once. Remove from the grill as they are done. Cut the squid tubes into 1 cm/½-inch rings.

5 Whisk the dressing again. In a large bowl combine the scallops, prawns, squid, chilli, 2 tablespoons of the parsley and half of the dressing; gently toss to coat. Arrange the salad leaves in a serving bowl and toss with the remaining dressing. Mound the seafood on top and garnish with the remaining parsley. Serve warm with lemon wedges.

SERVES: 4–6

NOTE!

To clean tender baby squid, cut off the tentacles and reserve, and then remove the beak if present. Cut off the head and discard. Insert your finger into the body and pull out the cartilage and squeeze out the insides. Keep the body intact for grilling.

SCALLOPS

WITH ITALIAN SALSA VERDE

PREP TIME: 20 minutes
GRILLING TIME: 3–4 minutes

SALSA VERDE

75 g/3 oz flat-leaf parsley
2 oil-packed anchovy fillets
2 tablespoons Dijon mustard
1 tablespoon capers, rinsed and drained
1 tablespoon white wine vinegar
1 garlic clove, finely chopped

Coarse salt
Freshly ground black pepper
Extra-virgin olive oil
12 large scallops, each about 50 g/2 oz

1 In a food processor combine the salsa verde ingredients, including ¼ teaspoon salt and ⅛ teaspoon pepper, and then pulse until the mixture is finely chopped. With the motor running, add 150 ml/¼ pint oil in a thin stream through the feed tube and continue processing until smooth and creamy, about 2 minutes.

2 Prepare the grill for direct cooking over high heat (230–290°C/450–550°F).

3 Pat the scallops dry. Remove and discard the small, tough side muscle that might be left on each one. Lightly coat the scallops on both sides with oil and season evenly with ½ teaspoon salt and ¼ teaspoon pepper. Grill the scallops over **grilling/direct high heat**, with the lid closed, until just opaque in the centre, 3–4 minutes, turning once.

4 Spoon a pool of sauce on each of four plates. Place the scallops on top of the sauce. Serve immediately.

SERVES: 4

NOTE!

Serve the scallops and sauce over wild rice or whole-grain barley.

SAUSAGE-STUFFED CALAMARI

WITH QUICK SAFFRON AIOLI

PREP TIME: 40 minutes
GRILLING TIME: 10–14 minutes
SPECIAL EQUIPMENT: perforated grill pan

AIOLI

⅛ teaspoon crumbled saffron threads (about 20 strands)
1½ tablespoons warm white wine
250 ml/8 fl oz mayonnaise
2 teaspoons fresh lemon juice
2 small garlic cloves, finely chopped
¼ teaspoon freshly ground black pepper

250 g/8 oz fresh hot Italian sausage, casings removed
2 garlic cloves, finely chopped
½ teaspoon smoked paprika
1 tablespoon coarsely chopped flat-leaf parsley
20 large, cleaned squid tubes, with their tentacles, rinsed and patted dry
Extra-virgin olive oil
¾ teaspoon coarse salt
¼ teaspoon freshly ground black pepper
Lemon wedges

1 In a little saucer soak the saffron threads in the warm wine for 20 minutes. Transfer the saffron-wine mixture to a small bowl and add the mayonnaise. Pour the lemon juice into the saffron-wine soaking saucer and swirl around to catch any remaining saffron essence; add to the mayonnaise along with the garlic and pepper. Whisk to blend.

2 In a medium bowl break up the sausage thoroughly with a fork. Fold in the garlic, paprika and parsley. Finely chop the squid tentacles and add to the bowl; mix with a fork until evenly blended. Using your fingers, pick up a pinch of stuffing at a time and gently press it into the opening at the top of each calamari tube, being careful as they can tear easily. Completely fill the tubes, as the calamari will shrink quite a bit as they cook.

3 Prepare the grill for direct cooking over high heat (230–290°C/450–550°F) and preheat a perforated grill pan for at least 10 minutes.

4 Lightly brush the calamari with oil and season evenly with the salt and pepper. Grill the calamari on the grill pan over **grilling/direct high heat** for 10–14 minutes, with the lid closed, until golden brown and firm and the sausage filling is cooked through, turning once (do not move the calamari for the first 5 minutes of cooking time on each side or they will stick). Remove from the grill and serve with the lemon wedges and aioli on the side.

SERVES: 4; 6 as an appetiser

MEAT

ITALIAN SAUSAGES

WITH LENTILS AND ROSEMARY

PREP TIME: 20 minutes, plus about 40 minutes for the lentils
GRILLING TIME: 8–12 minutes

175 g/6 oz dried brown lentils
2 sprigs fresh rosemary, each about 5 cm/2 inches long
1 bay leaf
1 tablespoon extra-virgin olive oil
1 large carrot, about 150 g/5 oz, cut into 5-mm/¼-inch dice
1 small onion, finely chopped
2 garlic cloves, finely chopped
350 ml/12 fl oz dry white wine
350 ml/12 fl oz chicken stock
1 tablespoon sherry wine vinegar
¾ teaspoon coarse salt
¼ teaspoon freshly ground black pepper
8 fresh Italian sausages with fennel, each 75–125 g/3–4 oz
2 tablespoons finely chopped flat-leaf parsley

1 Check the lentils for any small stones, and then place in a sieve; rinse under cold water. Place in a saucepan with one rosemary sprig and the bay leaf. Add enough water to cover the lentils by 5 cm/2 inches. Bring to the boil, and then reduce the heat to a simmer. Partially cover and cook for 18–20 minutes, until the lentils are tender but still firm to the bite, stirring occasionally (the lentils will continue to cook in the pan). Drain the lentils and discard the rosemary and bay leaf.

2 In a large frying pan over a medium heat, warm the oil. Add the carrot and onion and sauté for 3–5 minutes, until bright in colour and crisp-tender. Add the garlic and sauté until fragrant, about 1 minute. Add the wine and boil for about 2 minutes, until reduced by half. Add the stock, lentils and the remaining rosemary sprig. Simmer, uncovered, over a medium-low heat for 12–15 minutes, until the liquid is mostly absorbed and the lentils are soft but not mushy, stirring frequently. Add the vinegar, salt and black pepper and stir to combine. Discard the rosemary.

3 Prepare the grill for direct cooking over medium heat (180–230°C/350–450°F).

4 Grill the sausages over **grilling/direct medium heat** for 8–12 minutes, with the lid closed, until fully cooked (70°F/160°F), turning occasionally. (Thicker sausages may take a few extra minutes.) Spoon the lentils on to serving plates and top with the sausages. Garnish with the parsley. Serve immediately.

SERVES: 4

PORTUGUESE CALDO VERDE

PREP TIME: 15 minutes
GRILLING TIME: 41–45 minutes
SPECIAL EQUIPMENT: grill-proof cast-iron casserole

375 g/12 oz fully cooked Spanish chorizo sausage
1 tablespoon extra-virgin olive oil
1 Spanish onion, chopped
3 garlic cloves, finely chopped
½ teaspoon crushed chilli flakes
1.5 litres/2½ pints low-sodium chicken stock
375 g/12 oz salad potatoes, cut crossways into 1-cm/½-inch
    slices
1 bay leaf
1 teaspoon paprika
1 teaspoon coarse salt
½ teaspoon freshly ground black pepper
1 can (400 g/13 oz) cannellini beans, rinsed and drained
1 bunch green curly kale, tough ribs removed, leaves torn into
    bite-sized pieces

1 Prepare the grill for direct cooking over medium-low heat (about 180°C/350°F).

2 Grill the sausage over **grilling/direct medium-low heat** for 5–7 minutes, with the lid closed, until browned on all sides, turning as needed. When cool enough to handle, cut into 5-mm/¼-inch-thick slices.

3 In a grill-proof cast-iron casserole over **direct medium-low heat**, warm the oil. Add the onion and cook for about 3 minutes, with the grill lid closed, until softened, stirring frequently. Add the garlic and chilli flakes and cook until fragrant, about 1 minute, stirring constantly. Add the stock, potatoes, bay leaf, paprika, salt and pepper. Bring to the boil, and then simmer, with the pot partially covered and the grill lid closed for 25–30 minutes, until the potatoes are tender, stirring occasionally. Stir in the sausage, beans and kale and continue cooking until the kale wilts, 2–3 minutes, stirring frequently. Remove the bay leaf, ladle into bowls, and serve hot.

SERVES: 6–8

PORK PINCHITOS

PREP TIME: 20 minutes
MARINATING TIME: 6–12 hours
GRILLING TIME: 4–5 minutes
SPECIAL EQUIPMENT: 20–24 flat metal or bamboo skewers, each
    15–20 cm/6–8 inches long (if using bamboo, soak in water for
    at least 30 minutes)

MARINADE

75 ml/3 fl oz dry white wine
75 ml/3 fl oz extra-virgin olive oil
2 teaspoons smoked paprika
2 fresh bay leaves, torn into small pieces, or 1 dried bay leaf,
    crumbled
2 large garlic cloves, finely chopped
1 teaspoon coarse salt
¾ teaspoon ground black pepper
⅛ teaspoon crushed chilli flakes, or to taste

625 g/1¼ lb boneless pork, cut into 2.5-cm/1-inch cubes
1 lemon, cut into wedges

1 In a medium bowl whisk the marinade ingredients. Add the pork cubes and turn to coat evenly. Cover and refrigerate for at least 6 hours or up to 12 hours, turning occasionally.

2 If wished, fold a 30 cm/12-inch piece of aluminium foil lengthways into quarters to create a strip that will be placed directly on the cooking grates underneath the blunt ends of the skewers, preventing them from catching fire.

3 Prepare the grill for direct cooking over medium-high heat (200–260°C/400–500°F).

4 Transfer the pork cubes to a colander to drain while you assemble the skewers. Discard the marinade. Thread three or four cubes of pork on to each skewer, allowing the cubes to touch just barely. Dab the pork lightly with kitchen paper so the meat will sear nicely (do not dry the pork completely).

5 Place the blunt end of the skewers over the strip of foil, and then grill over **grilling/direct medium-high heat** for 4–5 minutes, with the lid closed, until the pork is golden brown and firm, turning once. Transfer the skewers to a serving plate. Squeeze some lemon juice on top and serve right away.

SERVES: 4

NOTE!

Search out pork with nice marbling, ideally from a local butcher. If there's any exterior fat, don't trim it off – it will add to the sizzle and flavour.

FRESH PORK SAUSAGES

WITH ROMESCO SAUCE

PREP TIME: 40 minutes
CHILLING TIME: at least 1 hour
GRILLING TIME: 10–12 minutes

SAUSAGES

500 g/1 lb lean minced pork
175 g/6 oz thin bacon rashers, diced
50 g/2 oz thinly sliced Parma ham, diced (optional)
2 spring onions, finely chopped (white and light green
    parts only)
2 teaspoons roughly chopped flat-leaf parsley
2 garlic cloves, finely chopped

Coarse salt
Freshly ground black pepper

SAUCE

2 slices coarse artisan bread, crusts removed, cut into cubes
3 tablespoons red wine vinegar
4 tablespoons flaked almonds
2 small garlic cloves
50 g/2 oz tomatoes, diced, with juice
1 piquillo pepper (from a jar)
1 teaspoon smoked paprika
Extra-virgin olive oil

1 Mix the sausage ingredients, including ½ teaspoon salt and ¼ teaspoon pepper, and then gently form 16–18 sausages of equal size, each 6–7 cm/2½–3 inches long. Cover and refrigerate until ready to grill.

2 In a small bowl combine the bread cubes and vinegar; turn to coat. Allow stand for about 10 minutes. In a small, dry frying pan over a medium heat, toast the almonds for 3–5 minutes, until just golden, watching carefully to prevent burning, shaking the pan frequently. Cool for 5 minutes. In a food processor with the motor running, drop the garlic cloves through the feed tube; process until the pieces stop moving. Add the almonds and pulse until grainy. Add the bread and vinegar mixture, tomatoes, piquillo pepper, paprika and ¼ teaspoon salt and process until well blended. With the motor running, add 4 tablespoons oil in a slow, steady stream and process just until smooth (stop the machine and scrape down the inside of the bowl midway through). Cover and refrigerate for at least 1 hour to allow the flavours to marry. Return to room temperature before serving.

3 Prepare the grill for direct cooking over medium-high heat (200–260°C/400–500°F).

4 Lightly coat the sausages with oil and season evenly with ¼ teaspoon salt and ⅛ teaspoon pepper. Grill over **grilling/direct medium-high heat** for 10–12 minutes, with the lid closed, until cooked to medium doneness (70°C/160°F), turning once. Serve warm with the sauce.

SERVES: 4

SHEFTALIA

WITH TAHINI SAUCE

PREP TIME: 30 minutes
GRILLING TIME: about 15 minutes

SHEFTALIA

625 g/1¼ lb minced pork (not lean), preferably pork shoulder
1 small onion, finely chopped
5 tablespoons finely chopped flat-leaf parsley
1 tablespoon finely chopped mint
1 tablespoon finely chopped oregano
1 tablespoon fresh lemon juice
1½ teaspoons coarse salt
½ teaspoon freshly ground black pepper

SAUCE

4 tablespoons tahini
4 tablespoons full-fat plain yogurt
2 tablespoons olive oil
2 tablespoons fresh lemon juice
1 teaspoon finely chopped garlic
½ teaspoon coarse salt
⅛ teaspoon ground cayenne pepper
2 tablespoons water

1 Mix the sheftalia ingredients, and then form into eight sausages, each 12–15cm/5–6 inches long and about 1.5 cm/¾ inch thick. Set aside at room temperature.

2 Prepare the grill for direct cooking over medium heat (180–230°C/350–450°F).

3 Grill the sausages over **grilling/direct medium heat** for about 15 minutes, with the lid closed, until browned and cooked to medium doneness (70°C/160°F), turning occasionally.

4 Whisk all the sauce ingredients, except the water, until blended. Then whisk in water, 1 tablespoon at a time, to create a thick, smooth, but not runny sauce.

5 Serve the sheftalia warm with the tahini sauce.

SERVES: 8

OREGANO-RUBBED VEAL CHOPS

WITH SPINACH ORZO

PREP TIME: 25 minutes
GRILLING TIME: 10–12 minutes

4 bone-in rib or loin veal chops, each about 375 g/12 oz and
    2.5 cm/1 inch thick
Extra-virgin olive oil
Coarse salt
Freshly ground black pepper
2 teaspoons dried oregano
250 g/8 oz dried orzo pasta
25 g/1 oz unsalted butter
2 shallots, finely chopped
2 teaspoons finely chopped garlic
125 g/4 oz baby spinach, roughly chopped
4 tablespoons toasted pine nuts
1 tablespoon finely grated lemon zest
2 teaspoons fresh lemon juice
½ teaspoon cracked black pepper

NOTE!

If you prefer to use boneless veal chops, decrease the cooking time by
a few minutes.

1 Lightly brush both sides of the chops with oil and season evenly with 1¼ teaspoons salt and ½ teaspoon pepper. Crumble the oregano in your fingers and massage about ¼ teaspoon into each side of each chop. Allow the chops to stand at room temperature for 15–30 minutes before grilling.

2 Prepare the grill for direct and indirect cooking over high heat (230–290°C/450–550°F).

3 In a large saucepan of generously salted, boiling water, cook the orzo for 9–10 minutes, until just tender but still firm to the bite. Drain well. Set aside.

4 In a small, dry frying pan over a medium heat, toast the pine nuts until they start to turn golden in spots, shaking the pan frequently. Remove from the heat and transfer the nuts to a plate to cool.

5 In a large nonstick frying pan over a medium heat, melt the butter with 1 tablespoon oil. Add the shallots and sauté for about 5 minutes, until tender and light golden. Add the garlic and sauté for 1 minute, stirring constantly. Add the drained orzo, spinach, pine nuts, lemon zest and juice and cracked black pepper; toss to blend. Season with ¾ teaspoon salt and, if liked, add more pepper. Cover and keep warm.

6 Grill the chops over **grilling/direct high heat** for about 5 minutes, with the lid closed, until marked by the grill, turning once. Move the chops over **roasting/indirect high heat**, close the lid, and continue cooking to your desired doneness, 5–7 minutes for medium rare. Serve the chops warm with spinach orzo on the side.

SERVES: 4

BISTECCA ALLA FIORENTINA

OVER ROCKET WITH SHAVED PARMESAN

PREP TIME: 15 minutes
GRILLING TIME: about 10 minutes

2 T-bone steaks, each 625–750 g/1¼–1½ lb and about
    3.5 cm/1½ inches thick, trimmed of excess fat
Extra-virgin olive oil
Coarse salt
Freshly ground black pepper
2 tablespoons finely chopped rosemary leaves
250 g/8 oz baby rocket
20 g/¾ oz Parmesan cheese, shaved
Juice of ½ lemon
1 whole lemon, cut into 4 wedges

1 Prepare the grill for direct cooking over high heat
(230–290°C/450–550°F).

2 Brush the steaks on both sides with 2 tablespoons oil,
generously season with salt and pepper, and then press
the rosemary into both sides of the steaks. Allow the steaks
to stand at room temperature for 30 minutes before grilling.

3 Grill the steaks over **grilling/direct high heat**, with the
lid closed, until cooked to your desired doneness, about
10 minutes for medium rare, turning occasionally. Remove
from the grill and allow to rest for 5 minutes.

4 In a bowl mix the rocket and cheese, drizzle with
1½ tablespoons oil, season with ¼ teaspoon salt
and a pinch of pepper, and toss well. Spread the rocket on
a large serving plate.

5 Cut the steaks into 1-cm/½-inch slices. Arrange the
slices in the centre of the rocket, slightly overlapping.
Pour any accumulated juices over the meat. Drizzle the steak
and rocket with oil and the juice of ½ lemon. Garnish with the
lemon wedges. Serve immediately.

SERVES: 4

The correct way to carve these steaks in the style of Florence is to first
separate the fillet and sirloin from the T-shaped bone. Then cut slices
across the meat as you see here.

LAMB AND ARTICHOKE SPIEDINI

WITH QUICK AIOLI

PREP TIME: 20 minutes
MARINATING TIME: 1 hour
GRILLING TIME: about 6 minutes
SPECIAL EQUIPMENT: 8–10 metal or bamboo skewers (if using
    bamboo, soak in water for at least 30 minutes)

MARINADE
2 teaspoons finely grated lemon zest
4 tablespoons fresh lemon juice
3 tablespoons extra-virgin olive oil
2 teaspoons finely chopped rosemary
1 large garlic clove, finely chopped

Coarse salt
Freshly ground black pepper
250 g/8 oz frozen artichoke hearts, thawed
750 g/1½ lb lamb from the leg or shoulder, trimmed, cut into
    1.5-cm/¾-inch cubes

AIOLI
150 ml/¼ pint mayonnaise
1 teaspoon finely grated lemon zest
2 teaspoons fresh lemon juice
1 garlic clove, finely chopped

Lemon wedges

1 In a medium bowl whisk the marinade ingredients, including 1 teaspoon salt and ½ teaspoon pepper. Cut the artichoke hearts lengthways in half or into quarters (the pieces should be wide enough to skewer, but not wider than the lamb cubes). Add the artichokes and lamb cubes to the marinade and turn gently to coat. Allow to stand at room temperature for 1 hour, stirring occasionally.

2 In a bowl whisk the aioli ingredients, including a pinch of salt and pepper.

3 Prepare the grill for direct cooking over medium-high heat (200–260°C/400–500°F).

4 Thread the lamb and artichokes on to each skewer as follows: one artichoke heart, three lamb cubes, one artichoke heart, three lamb cubes, and one artichoke heart (the lamb cubes should barely touch). Grill the skewers over **grilling/direct medium-high heat**, with the lid closed, until browned and just firm to the touch, about 6 minutes for medium rare, turning once or twice. Serve warm with lemon wedges.

SERVES: 4

CHERMOULA-MARINATED LEG OF LAMB

WITH ALMOND COUSCOUS

PREP TIME: 30 minutes
MARINATING TIME: 4–24 hours
GRILLING TIME: 20–30 minutes

MARINADE

4 garlic cloves, finely chopped
4 tablespoons flat-leaf parsley
4 tablespoons mint leaves
4 tablespoons full-fat Greek yogurt
2 tablespoons fresh lemon juice
1 teaspoon ground cumin
1 teaspoon ground paprika
1 teaspoon ground coriander
¼ teaspoon ground cayenne pepper

Extra-virgin olive oil
Coarse salt
1 boneless leg of lamb, 1.75–2 kg/3½–4 lb, butterflied,
     trimmed of excess fat
1 small red pepper, finely chopped
1 small garlic clove, finely chopped
¼ teaspoon saffron threads
250 g/8 oz couscous
350 ml/12 fl oz chicken stock
4 tablespoons toasted almonds, roughly chopped
2 tablespoons finely chopped fresh coriander

1 In the bowl of a food processor, combine the garlic, parsley and mint. Pulse to coarsely chop. Add the remaining marinade ingredients, including 4 tablespoons oil and 2 teaspoons salt, and pulse to blend. Spread the marinade all over the lamb and in the folds of the meat. Place in a baking dish and cover with clingfilm. Refrigerate for 4–24 hours. Allow the lamb to stand at room temperature for 30 minutes before grilling.

2 Prepare the grill for direct cooking over medium heat (180–230°C/350–450°F).

3 Grill the lamb over **grilling/direct medium heat**, with the lid closed, until cooked to your desired doneness, 20–30 minutes for medium rare, turning occasionally. Remove from the grill and allow to rest for 15 minutes.

4 In a saucepan over a medium heat, warm 1 tablespoon oil. Add the pepper, garlic and saffron and sauté for about 1 minute, until fragrant. Add the couscous and stir to coat. Add the stock and ¾ teaspoon salt. Bring to the boil, and then cover the saucepan and remove from the heat. Leave to stand for 5–10 minutes, until the liquid is absorbed. Fluff the couscous with a fork and stir in the almonds and coriander. Drizzle with some additional olive oil.

5 Cut the lamb into slices and serve with the couscous.

SERVES: 6–8

GIGOT DE SEPT HEURES

PREP TIME: 20 minutes
SOAKING TIME: 18 hours
GRILLING TIME: about 4 hours
SPECIAL EQUIPMENT: grill-proof cast-iron casserole, fat separator, muslin, kitchen string

600 g/1 lb 3 oz dried cannellini beans
3 litres/5 pints water
1 boneless leg of lamb, 1.5–1.75 kg/3–3½ lb, rolled and tied
Extra-virgin olive oil
Coarse salt
Freshly ground black pepper
8 garlic cloves, peeled
2 large carrots, cut into 5-cm/2-inch chunks
1 onion, quartered
6 fresh rosemary sprigs
6 fresh thyme sprigs
4 bay leaves
1 bottle (750 ml/1¼ pints) dry white wine
15 g/½ oz unsalted butter

BEANS

2 fresh rosemary sprigs
10 black peppercorns
2 whole cloves
1 bay leaf
6 garlic cloves, peeled and smashed but still intact
2.2 litres/3¾ pints water
125 ml/4 fl oz chicken stock, plus more if needed
2 tablespoons extra-virgin olive oil
15 g/½ oz unsalted butter

1 Soak the beans overnight in 3 litres/5 pints of water.

2 Rub the lamb with oil and season evenly and generously with salt and pepper. Allow the lamb to stand at room temperature for 30 minutes before grilling.

3 Prepare the grill for direct and indirect cooking over medium-high heat (200–260°C/400–500°F).

4 Grill the lamb over **grilling/direct medium-high heat** for 10–12 minutes, with the lid closed, until browned on all sides, turning as needed. Remove from the grill.

5 Place the garlic, carrots, onion, rosemary, thyme and bay leaves in a grill-proof cast-iron casserole. Place the lamb on top of the vegetables and herbs. Add the wine. Place the casserole over **grilling/direct medium-high heat**, close the grill lid, and bring the wine to the boil. Reduce the heat of the grill to low (as close to 150°C/300°F as possible), move the casserole over indirect heat, cover the casserole, close the grill lid, and cook over **roasting/indirect low heat** for 3–4 hours, until the lamb is tender and falling apart, turning the meat every hour. Remove the casserole from the grill and transfer the lamb to a chopping board. Pull the lamb apart into chunks. Reserve the carrots and onion and strain the braising liquid through a fat separator. Allow to stand until the fat rises to the surface. Discard the fat and solids. Transfer the liquid to a saucepan and cook over a medium heat for about 10 minutes, until reduced by half. Put the lamb in the saucepan and turn to coat in the liquid.

6 Two hours before the lamb is finished, prepare the beans. Create a bouquet garni by wrapping the rosemary sprigs, peppercorns, cloves and bay leaf in a piece of muslin and tying with kitchen string. Drain the beans and rinse under cold water. In a large saucepan combine the beans, garlic, bouquet garni and water. Bring to the boil over a high heat, and then reduce the heat to low. Cover the pan and simmer for 30–40 minutes, until the beans are tender.

7 Remove and discard the bouquet garni, and drain the beans. Place the beans in a food processor. Add 125ml/ 4 fl oz chicken stock, the oil, butter, 2 teaspoons salt and ½ teaspoon pepper and process until smooth. If the beans are too thick, add additional chicken stock and process to your desired consistency.

8 Spread the beans on a serving plate and top with the meat and reserved carrots and onion. Serve warm.

SERVES: 6–8

LAMB LOIN CHOPS

WITH MINT PESTO

PREP TIME: 15 minutes
MARINATING TIME: 15–30 minutes
GRILLING TIME: 8–10 minutes

MARINADE

2 tablespoons extra-virgin olive oil
1 teaspoon coarse salt
½ teaspoon freshly ground black pepper
1 garlic clove, finely chopped

8 lamb loin chops, each about 3 cm/1¼ inches thick, trimmed of
    excess fat

PESTO

25 g/1 oz basil leaves
50 g/2 oz mint leaves
4 tablespoons finely grated Parmesan cheese
4 tablespoons walnuts
1 tablespoon fresh lemon juice
2 garlic cloves
½ teaspoon coarse salt
4 tablespoons extra-virgin olive oil

1 Whisk the marinade ingredients. Arrange the chops in a single layer in a rimmed baking dish. Coat the lamb on both sides with the marinade, rubbing it in. Allow the lamb to stand at room temperature for 15–30 minutes before grilling.

2 Place all the pesto ingredients, except the oil, in a food processor or blender and process to combine. Then, with the motor running, slowly add the oil to make a thin paste. Pour into a serving bowl, cover, and leave to stand at room temperature until ready to serve.

3 Prepare the grill for direct cooking over high heat (230–290°C/450–550°F).

4 Grill the lamb over **grilling/direct high heat**, with the lid closed, until cooked to your desired doneness, 8–10 minutes for medium rare, turning once. Remove from the grill and allow to rest for 3–5 minutes. Serve the chops warm with the pesto spooned on top.

SERVES: 4

ITALIAN BEEF SANDWICHES

WITH PICKLED VEGETABLES

PREP TIME: 25 minutes
GRILLING TIME: 9–11 minutes

RUB
1 teaspoon dried oregano
1 teaspoon dried thyme
³/₄ teaspoon sea salt
¹/₂ teaspoon ground black pepper
¹/₄ teaspoon garlic granules

1 piece of skirt steak, 750 g–1 kg/1¹/₂–2 lb and about
    1.5 cm/³/₄ inch thick
Extra-virgin olive oil
500 ml/17 fl oz beef stock
125 ml/4 fl oz dry red wine
1 garlic clove, thinly sliced
Sea salt
Ground black pepper
6 ciabatta rolls, each about 15 cm/6 inches long, split
1 jar (475 ml/16 fl oz) pickled Italian vegetables (giardiniera),
    drained and thinly sliced

1. In a small bowl mix the rub ingredients. Lightly brush the steak on both sides with oil and season evenly with the rub. Allow the steak to stand at room temperature for 15–30 minutes before grilling.

2. Prepare the grill for direct cooking over medium heat (180–230°C/350–450°F).

3. In a saucepan over a high heat, bring the stock, wine and garlic to a simmer. Reduce the heat to low and cook for 15 minutes. Season with salt and pepper. Keep warm.

4. Brush the cooking grates clean. Grill the steak over **grilling/direct medium heat**, with the lid closed as much as possible, until cooked to your desired doneness, 8–10 minutes for medium rare, turning once or twice (if flare-ups occur, move the steak temporarily over indirect heat). Transfer to a chopping board and leave to rest for 3–5 minutes.

5. While the steak rests, toast the rolls, cut sides down, over **grilling/direct medium heat**, for 30 seconds–1 minute.

6. Pour the broth into six small serving bowls or ramekins. Cut the steak in half lengthways and then cut across the grain into thin slices. Pile the bottom of each toasted roll with steak and some pickled vegetables. Cut each sandwich in half crossways. Serve warm with the broth for dipping.

SERVES: 6

FILLET STEAKS

WITH GARLICKY PRAWNS

PREP TIME: 10 minutes
GRILLING TIME: 17–19 minutes

4 fillet steaks, each about 250 g/8 oz and 3.5 cm/1½ inches
    thick
Extra-virgin olive oil
2½ teaspoons sea salt
½ teaspoon ground black pepper
125 g/4 oz unsalted butter
2 large garlic cloves, coarsely chopped
12 raw tiger prawns, peeled and deveined, tails left on
Finely grated zest of 1 lemon
¼ teaspoon crushed chilli flakes
2 tablespoons chopped flat-leaf parsley

1 Lightly brush the steaks on both sides with oil and season evenly with 2 teaspoons of the salt and the pepper. Allow the steaks to stand at room temperature for 15–30 minutes before grilling.

2 Prepare the grill for direct cooking over medium heat (180–230°C/350–450°F).

3 In a small saucepan over a medium heat, heat the butter and garlic until the butter melts and comes to the boil. Remove from the heat and allow to stand for 5 minutes.

4 Place the prawns in a bowl and toss with 2 tablespoons of the garlic butter; reserve the remaining butter. Season the prawns with the lemon zest, the remaining ½ teaspoon salt and the chilli flakes.

5 Brush the cooking grates clean. Grill the steaks over **grilling/direct medium heat**, with the lid closed as much as possible, until cooked to your desired doneness, 12–14 minutes for medium rare, turning once or twice (if flare-ups occur, move the steaks temporarily over indirect heat). Remove from the grill and leave to rest for 3–5 minutes.

6 Grill the prawns over **grilling/direct medium heat** for about 5 minutes, with the lid closed as much as possible, until they are firm to the touch, lightly charred, and just turning opaque in the centre, turning once.

7 Reheat the butter. Serve the steaks warm topped with prawns, butter and parsley.

SERVES: 4

BALSAMIC-MARINATED SKIRT STEAKS

WITH GRILLED SMASHED POTATOES AND OLIVE AIOLI

PREP TIME: 15 minutes, plus about 30 minutes for the potatoes
MARINATING TIME: 30 minutes–2 hours
GRILLING TIME: 4–6 minutes

MARINADE

75 ml/3 fl oz balsamic vinegar
4 tablespoons extra-virgin olive oil
4 tablespoons chopped rosemary leaves

1 kg/2 lb skirt steak, 0.5–1.5 cm/½–¾ inch thick, trimmed of
    excess surface fat, cut into long strips

POTATOES

Sea salt
500 g/1 lb red or white new potatoes, each about the size of
    a golf ball
2 tablespoons extra-virgin olive oil
Ground black pepper

AIOLI

125 ml/4 fl oz good-quality mayonnaise
1 tablespoon black olive tapenade
1 teaspoon fresh lemon juice
1 teaspoon finely chopped garlic

1 In a large glass or stainless-steel bowl, whisk the marinade ingredients. Place the steaks in the bowl, turn, and rub the marinade in with your fingertips to coat all sides of the meat. Cover and refrigerate for at least 30 minutes or up to 2 hours.

2 Fill a large saucepan with water and add enough salt so it tastes like seawater (250 g/8 oz salt to 2 litres/3½ pints water). Add the potatoes and bring to the boil. Cook until tender, 20–30 minutes, depending on the size of the potatoes. Drain, and allow the potatoes to rest until they are cool enough to handle. Use the bottom of a small saucepan and gently press on each potato to smash it to an even thickness, about 1.5 cm/¾ inch thick. Brush both sides with oil and season with salt and pepper.

3 In a medium bowl mix the aioli ingredients. Cover and refrigerate until serving.

4 Prepare the grill for direct cooking over high heat (230–290°C/450–550°F).

5 Remove the steaks from the bowl and discard the marinade. Pat the steaks dry with kitchen paper and season evenly with salt and pepper. Brush the cooking grates clean. Grill the steaks over **grilling/direct high heat**, with the lid closed as much as possible, until cooked to your desired doneness, 4–6 minutes for medium rare, turning once or twice (if flare-ups occur, move the steaks temporarily over indirect heat). Grill the potatoes while you grill the steaks, and cook them until they begin to brown and crisp, about 5 minutes, turning once. Allow the steaks rest for 3–5 minutes. Cut the steaks across the grain into 5-mm/¼-inch thick slices, and serve with the potatoes and the aioli.

SERVES: 4

NOTE!

Boil the potatoes first, smash them under a pan and then grill them along with the steaks until brown and crispy.

T-BONE STEAKS

WITH BÈARNAISE SAUCE

PREP TIME: 15 minutes
GRILLING TIME: 6–8 minutes

2 T-bone steaks, each about 625 g/1¼ lb and 2.5 cm/1 inch
    thick, trimmed of excess fat
Extra-virgin olive oil
Sea salt
Ground black pepper

SAUCE

3 tablespoons dry white wine
3 tablespoons white wine vinegar
1 shallot, finely chopped
3 egg yolks (see note below)
175 g/6 oz unsalted butter, melted
¼ teaspoon sea salt
1 teaspoon ground black pepper
2 tablespoons finely chopped tarragon

1 Lightly brush the steaks on both sides with oil and season evenly with salt and pepper. Allow the steaks to stand at room temperature for 15–30 minutes before grilling.

2 Prepare the grill for direct cooking over high heat (230–290°C/450–550°F).

3 In a small saucepan over a high heat, bring the wine, vinegar, and shallot to the boil for about 2 minutes. Cook until the liquid is reduced to about 2 tablespoons. Strain through a sieve into a small bowl; reserve the vinegar mixture and discard the shallot.

4 Place the yolks in a blender. With the machine running on high, drizzle in the vinegar mixture through the hole in the blender lid. Pouring in a slow stream, gradually add the melted butter. The sauce should be thick and have the consistency of mayonnaise. Season with the salt and pepper. Transfer the sauce to a small heat-proof bowl. Stir in the tarragon. Place the bowl over a pan of very hot, but not simmering, water to keep the sauce warm while grilling the steaks.

5 Brush the cooking grates clean. Grill the steaks over **grilling/direct high heat**, with the lid closed as much as possible, until cooked to your desired doneness, 6–8 minutes for medium rare, turning once or twice (if flare-ups occur, move the steaks temporarily over indirect heat). Remove from the grill and allow to rest for 3–5 minutes. Cut the steaks into slices, and arrange the slices on serving plates. Serve warm with the sauce.

SERVES: 4

NOTE!

Using raw egg yolks to make béarnaise sauce could cause salmonella poisoning. To avoid that risk, use yolks from pasteurised eggs.

STEAK AND CHERRY TOMATO KEBABS

WITH CREAMY POLENTA

PREP TIME: 20 minutes
MARINATING TIME: 1–4 hours
GRILLING TIME: 6–8 minutes
SPECIAL EQUIPMENT: 12 metal or bamboo skewers (if using bamboo, soak in water for at least 30 minutes)

MARINADE

4 tablespoons extra-virgin olive oil
2 tablespoons choppedrosemary leaves
1 teaspoon crushed chilli flakes
1 teaspoon ground black pepper

750 g/1½ lb rump steak, 2.5–3 cm/1–1¼ inches thick, cut into 3.5-cm/1½-inch cubes

POLENTA

750 ml–1 litre/1¼–1½ pints full-fat milk or water
2 teaspoons sea salt
100 g/3½ oz dry polenta
25 g/1 oz unsalted butter
2½ teaspoons sea salt
750 g/1½ lb large cherry tomatoes
Extra-virgin olive oil

1 In a medium bowl whisk the marinade ingredients. Add the meat and turn to coat evenly. Cover the bowl and refrigerate for 1–4 hours.

2 In a saucepan over a high heat, bring 750 ml/1¼ pints of the milk to a simmer (do not boil). Add the salt, reduce the heat to medium-low, and add the polenta in a thin stream, whisking constantly to prevent the polenta from clumping. Bring back to a simmer, reduce the heat to low and continue cooking, whisking frequently, until the polenta is cooked and has a loose, porridge-like consistency. Stir in the butter, turn off the heat, and set aside.

3 Prepare the grill for direct cooking over high heat (230–290°C/450–550°F).

4 Remove the meat from the bowl and discard the marinade. Season evenly with the salt. Thread the meat on to skewers and the tomatoes on to their own skewers. Lightly brush the tomatoes with oil.

5 Brush the cooking grates clean. Grill the meat kebabs over **grilling/direct high heat**, with the lid closed as much as possible, until cooked to your desired doneness, 6–8 minutes for medium rare, turning once or twice (if flare-ups occur, move the kebabs temporarily over indirect heat). At the same time, grill the tomato kebabs over **grilling/direct high heat** for 3–4 minutes, until lightly charred and heated through, turning occasionally. Remove the kebabs from the grill as they are done.

6 If the polenta has cooled, place it over a medium heat until it is warmed through, adding 125–250 ml/4–8 fl oz milk, if necessary, stirring frequently. Serve the kebabs warm with the polenta.

SERVES: 4

SKIRT STEAKS

WITH GRUYÈRE-SHALLOT FONDUE

PREP TIME: 30 minutes
GRILLING TIME: 10–14 minutes

STEAKS

4 skirt steaks, each 175–250 g/6–8 oz and 3.5–5cm/
    1½–2 inches thick
2 teaspoons extra-virgin olive oil
2 teaspoons sea salt
¾ teaspoon ground black pepper

FONDUE

15 g/½ oz unsalted butter
1 shallot, finely chopped
4 tablespoons dry white wine
4 tablespoons beef stock
1 teaspoon white wine vinegar
250 g/8 oz Gruyère cheese, grated
1 tablespoon cornflour
1 tablespoon cognac or brandy
¾ teaspoon chopped thyme leaves
1 teaspoon ground black pepper
4 fresh thyme sprigs for garnish (optional)

1 Prepare the grill for direct cooking over medium heat (180–230°C/350–450°F).

2 Lightly brush the steaks on both sides with the oil and season evenly with the salt and pepper. Allow the steaks to stand at room temperature for 15–30 minutes before grilling.

3 In a saucepan over a medium heat, melt the butter. Add the shallot and cook for about 2 minutes, until tender, stirring occasionally. Add the wine, stock and vinegar, and bring to the boil over a high heat. Remove from the heat and set aside.

4 Brush the cooking grates clean. Grill the steaks over **grilling/direct medium heat**, with the lid closed as much as possible, until cooked to your desired doneness, 10–14 minutes for medium rare, turning once or twice (if flare-ups occur, move the steaks temporarily over indirect heat). Remove from the grill and allow to rest while finishing the fondue.

5 In a medium bowl toss the cheese and cornflour together. Return the wine mixture to the boil over a high heat. Reduce the heat to low. Stirring constantly, add the cheese to the wine mixture a handful at a time. Let each addition melt completely before adding the next. Cook just until the fondue comes to the boil. Stir in the cognac, thyme and pepper. Remove from the heat.

6 Transfer each steak to an individual plate. Top each with equal amounts of the fondue and a thyme sprig, if using. Serve warm. Serving suggestion: asparagus (for recipe, see page 175).

SERVES: 4

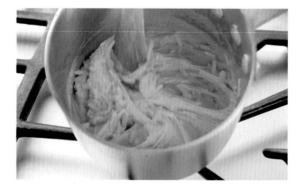

NOTE!

You will have the smoothest fondue if you melt the cheese one handful at a time and stir, stir, stir.

POULTRY

CHICKEN TAGINE

WITH PEPPERS, APRICOTS AND SAFFRON

PREP TIME: 15 minutes
GRILLING TIME: 1 hour 40 minutes
SPECIAL EQUIPMENT: grill-proof cast-iron casserole

8 chicken thighs (with bone and skin), each 250–275 g/8–9 oz
Extra-virgin olive oil
Coarse salt
Freshly ground black pepper
1 red onion, finely chopped
1 large red pepper, finely chopped
2 teaspoons finely chopped garlic
1 teaspoon ground coriander
1 teaspoon ground ginger
1/2 teaspoon ground cinnamon
1/2 teaspoon ground cumin
1/4 teaspoon saffron threads
175 g/6 oz dried apricots
75 g/3 oz pitted green olives, each cut in half
500 ml/17 fl oz chicken stock
125 ml/4 fl oz dry white wine

1 Prepare the grill for direct and indirect cooking over medium heat (180–230°C/350–450°F).

2 Lightly coat the chicken thighs with 2 tablespoons oil, season evenly with 1½ teaspoons salt and ¾ teaspoon pepper, and then grill over **grilling/direct medium heat** for about 4 minutes, with the lid closed, until well marked and lightly browned, turning once. Move over indirect heat.

3 Set a grill-proof cast-iron casserole over **grilling/direct medium heat** for about 4–5 minutes. Add 2 tablespoons oil, the onion and pepper and cook until softened, stirring often. Stir in the garlic, coriander, ginger, cinnamon, cumin, saffron, 1 teaspoon salt and ½ teaspoon pepper and cook until aromatic, about 30 seconds.

4 Add the apricots and olives and cook for 30 seconds, stirring constantly. Pour in the stock and wine, and scrape up any browned bits on the bottom of the casserole. Nestle the chicken into the sauce and bring to a simmer.

5 Cover the casserole, move it over **roasting/indirect medium heat** (keep the temperature of the grill between 220 and 230°C/425 and 450°F), and close the grill lid. Cook until the chicken is tender and the sauce is thickened, about 1½ hours, occasionally spooning some sauce over the chicken. (Check the casserole oven occasionally. If the lid doesn't fit securely, the sauce may dry out. If needed, stir in extra stock to compensate.) Remove from the grill and allow to stand at room temperature for 10 minutes to blend the flavours before serving.

SERVES: 4

CHICKEN CACCIATORE

PREP TIME: 20 minutes
MARINATING TIME: 2–4 hours
GRILLING TIME: about 1 hour
SPECIAL EQUIPMENT: 30-cm/2-inch cast-iron frying pan or 6-litre/
    10-pint grill-proof casserole

MARINADE

4 tablespoons extra-virgin olive oil
1 teaspoon paprika
1 teaspoon coarse salt
$\frac{1}{2}$ teaspoon freshly ground black pepper
1 garlic clove, finely chopped

4 chicken breasts (with bone and skin), each 300–375 g/
    10–12 oz
2 peppers, 1 red and 1 green
1 tablespoon extra-virgin olive oil
1 onion, finely chopped
3 garlic cloves, finely chopped
1 teaspoon dried oregano
$\frac{1}{2}$ teaspoon crushed chilli flakes
250 ml/8 fl oz dry white wine
2 cans (400 g/13 oz) Italian plum tomatoes in juice
125 ml/4 fl oz cup chicken stock
4 tablespoons tomato purée
1 bay leaf
1 teaspoon granulated sugar
$1\frac{1}{2}$ teaspoons coarse salt
1 teaspoon freshly ground black pepper

1 Whisk the marinade ingredients. Place the chicken breasts in a large, resealable plastic bag and pour in the marinade. Press the air out of the bag and seal tightly. Turn the bag to distribute the marinade, place in a bowl, and refrigerate for 2–4 hours.

2 Prepare the grill for direct and indirect cooking over medium heat (180–230°C/350–450°F).

3 Grill the peppers over **grilling/direct medium heat** for 10–12 minutes, with the lid closed, until blackened and blistered all over, turning occasionally. Put the peppers in a bowl and cover with clingfilm to trap the steam. Allow to stand for about 10 minutes. Remove from the bowl, peel away and discard the charred skin, cut off and discard the stalks and seeds, and then roughly chop the peppers.

4 Place a 30-cm/12-inch cast-iron frying pan over **grilling/ direct medium heat** (keep the temperature of the grill as close to 180°C/350°F as possible), and warm the oil. Add the onion and cook for about 3 minutes until softened, stirring frequently. Add the garlic, oregano and chilli flakes and cook for about 1 minute, until fragrant, stirring often. Add the wine and cook for about 6 minutes, until reduced by half, stirring once or twice. Add the peppers, tomatoes, stock, tomato purée, bay leaf, sugar, salt and pepper. Bring to the boil over **grilling/ direct medium heat** and cook for 6–8 minutes, until slightly thickened. Slide the pan over indirect heat. Keep the lid closed as much as possible during grilling.

5 Remove the chicken from the bag and discard the marinade. Grill the chicken, skin side down first, over **grilling/direct medium heat** for 5–7 minutes, with the lid closed, until the skin is golden brown, turning once. Transfer the chicken to the pan, skin side up, without submerging the skin. Cook over **roasting/indirect medium heat** for 20–30 minutes more, with the lid closed, until the chicken is thoroughly cooked. Remove the bay leaf and serve warm.

SERVES: 4

NOTE!

This Italian hunter's stew is redolent with tomatoes and spices. Be sure to use bone-in chicken breasts, which will allow the chicken to braise longer in the liquid without drying out. And don't submerge the chicken in the stock – keep the skin exposed to prevent it from becoming soggy while braising.

BALSAMIC CHICKEN BREASTS

WITH GRAPES, OLIVES AND ROSEMARY

PREP TIME: 10 minutes
GRILLING TIME: 18–21 minutes
SPECIAL EQUIPMENT: 30-cm/12-inch cast-iron frying pan

1 small garlic clove, finely chopped
Extra-virgin olive oil
Coarse salt
Freshly ground black pepper
4 boneless chicken breasts (with skin), each about
    250 g/8 oz
200 g/7 oz seedless red and/or green grapes
175 g/6 oz pitted Kalamata olives
2 sprigs fresh rosemary, each about 5 cm/2 inches long
125 g/4 fl oz balsamic vinegar

1 Prepare the grill for direct and indirect cooking over medium heat (180–230°C/350–450°F) and preheat a 30-cm/12-inch cast-iron frying pan over direct heat for 10 minutes.

2 In a small bowl whisk the garlic, 2 tablespoons oil, 1 teaspoon salt and ½ teaspoon pepper. Rub the seasoned oil all over the chicken and under the skin.

3 In a large bowl combine 150 g/5 oz of the grapes, the olives, rosemary, 1 tablespoon oil, ½ teaspoon salt and ¼ teaspoon pepper. Pour into the cast-iron pan. Cook over **grilling/direct medium heat**, with the lid closed, for 5 minutes, stirring frequently. Carefully slide the pan over **roasting/indirect medium heat** and continue cooking there while you grill the chicken, stirring occasionally.

4 Grill the chicken on the cooking grates, skin side down first, over **grilling/direct medium heat** for 4–5 minutes, with the lid closed, until the skin is golden brown and releases easily from the grates. Turn and grill 2 minutes more.

5 Nestle the chicken in the pan, skin side up, between the grapes and olives. Cook over **roasting/indirect medium heat** for 5–6 minutes, with the lid closed, until the meat is firm to the touch and opaque all the way to the centre. Transfer the chicken to a plate.

6 Return the pan over **grilling/direct medium heat**. Carefully add the vinegar and the remaining grapes. Cook over **grilling/direct medium heat** for 2–3 minutes, with the lid closed, until the sauce is slightly thickened and reduced, stirring frequently. Discard the rosemary sprigs. Serve the chicken warm with the sauce.

SERVES: 4

CHICKEN PAILLARDS

WITH CAPER-LEMON BUTTER SAUCE

PREP TIME: 20 minutes
MARINATING TIME: 30 minutes
GRILLING TIME: 4–6 minutes

4 boneless, skinless chicken breasts, each about 175 g/6 oz
1½ tablespoons extra-virgin olive oil
1 tablespoon white wine vinegar
1 teaspoon chopped oregano
½ teaspoon finely chopped anchovy fillet or anchovy
    paste (optional)
Coarse salt
Freshly ground black pepper
2 shallots, finely chopped
75 ml/3 fl oz dry white wine
3 tablespoons fresh lemon juice
75 ml/3 fl oz chicken stock
3 tablespoons capers, rinsed and drained
40–50 g/1½–2 oz cold salted butter, cut into 3–4 chunks
4 tablespoons finely chopped flat-leaf parsley

1 Place each chicken breast between two sheets of clingfilm and pound gently with a mallet to an even 1-cm/½-inch thickness, pounding out from the centre and being careful not to tear any holes. In a baking dish mix the oil, vinegar, oregano, anchovy, ½ teaspoon salt and ¼ teaspoon pepper. Add the chicken and brush all sides with the mixture. Cover and refrigerate for 30 minutes.

2 In a small saucepan add the shallot, wine and lemon juice. Bring to a simmer over a medium-high heat and cook for 2–4 minutes, until the liquid is reduced by about three-quarters. Add the stock and simmer for 2 minutes more; remove from the heat.

3 Prepare the grill for direct cooking over medium-high heat (200–230°C/400–450°F).

4 Grill the chicken over **grilling/direct medium-high heat**, for 4–6 minutes with the lid closed, until firm to the touch, golden, and no longer pink in the centre, turning once. Remove from the grill and cover with aluminium foil. Place the saucepan with the shallot mixture back over a medium-high heat and, when it's steaming, add the capers and butter. Shake and swirl the pan vigorously until the butter melts and thickens the mixture slightly. Remove from the heat and season with salt and pepper. Serve the chicken with the sauce spooned on top, garnished with parsley.

SERVES: 4

BRINED AND ROASTED CHICKEN

WITH OREGANO AND TARRAGON

PREP TIME: 15 minutes
BRINING TIME: 6–8 hours
GRILLING TIME: 1¼–1½ hours
SPECIAL EQUIPMENT: kitchen string, instant-read thermometer

BRINE

1 litre/1¾ pints water
125 g/4 oz sea salt
Juice of 2 lemons
2 tablespoons dried oregano
2 tablespoons dried tarragon
1 tablespoon garlic granules
2 teaspoons ground black pepper

3 litres/5 pints ice cubes
1 whole chicken, 2–2.5 kg/4–5 lb, giblets and any excess
   fat removed
1 tablespoon extra-virgin olive oil

1 In a large saucepan over a medium heat, combine the brine ingredients. Bring to a simmer and stir to dissolve the salt. Add the ice to the pan. Let the liquid cool to room temperature.

2 Submerge the chicken in the brine, with the breast facing down. Refrigerate the chicken in the saucepan for 6–8 hours.

3 Prepare the grill for indirect cooking over medium heat (about 200°C/400°F).

4 Remove the chicken from the brine. Discard the brine. Pat the chicken dry with kitchen paper. Lightly coat the outside of the chicken with the oil. Truss the chicken with kitchen string.

5 Brush the cooking grates clean. Grill the chicken, breast side up, over **roasting/indirect medium heat** for 1¼–1½ hours, with the lid closed, until the juices run clear and the internal temperature reaches 77°C/170°F in the thickest part of the thigh (not touching the bone), rotating the chicken as needed for even cooking and browning. Remove from the grill and allow to rest for 5–10 minutes (the internal temperature will rise 5–10 degrees during this time). Cut into serving pieces and serve warm.

SERVES: 4

ROSEMARY CHICKEN UNDER BRICKS

WITH GRILLED LEMONS

PREP TIME: 20 minutes
MARINATING TIME: 2–4 hours
GRILLING TIME: about 1 hour
SPECIAL EQUIPMENT: poultry shears; roasting tray and 2 foil-wrapped bricks or cast-iron frying pan; instant-read thermometer

MARINADE
4 tablespoons extra-virgin olive oil
4 tablespoons fresh lemon juice
1 tablespoon finely chopped rosemary leaves
2 teaspoons sea salt
3 garlic cloves, finely chopped

1 whole chicken, 2–2.5 kg/4–5 lb, giblets and any excess fat removed
2 lemons, halved
Extra-virgin olive oil

1 Whisk the marinade ingredients in a 33 x 23-cm/13 x 9-inch glass baking dish.

2 Place the chicken, breast side down, on a chopping board. Using poultry shears, cut from the neck to the tail end, along either side of the backbone, to remove it.

3 Once the backbone is out, you'll be able to see the interior of the chicken. Make a small slit in the cartilage at the bottom end of the breastbone. Then, placing both hands on the rib cage, crack the chicken open like a book. Run your fingers along either side of the cartilage in between the breast to loosen it from the flesh. Grab the bone and pull up on it to remove it along with the attached cartilage. The chicken should now lie flat.

4 Place the chicken in the dish and turn to coat it evenly with the marinade. Cover with clingfilm and refrigerate for 2–4 hours, turning occasionally.

5 Prepare the grill for direct cooking over medium-low heat (about 180°C/350°F).

6 Brush the cooking grates clean. Place the chicken, bone side down, over **grilling/direct medium-low heat**. Place the roasting tray on top of the chicken and weight it down with 2 bricks wrapped in foil (or use a cast-iron frying pan). Close the lid and cook for 20–30 minutes. Wearing barbecue mitts, remove the weight, turn the chicken over, replace the weight, close the lid, and cook for 20–30 minutes, until the juices run clear and the internal temperature reaches 77°C/170°F in the thickest part of the thigh (not touching the bone). Remove from the grill and allow to rest for 3–5 minutes (the internal temperature will rise 5–10 degrees during this time).

7 Brush the cut sides of the lemons with oil and grill over direct medium-low heat for about 5 minutes, until well charred and caramelised. Cut the chicken into serving pieces, squeeze the lemons over the chicken, and serve warm.

SERVES: 4

CHICKEN SALTIMBOCCA

IN WHITE WINE-BUTTER SAUCE

PREP TIME: 15 minutes, plus about 20 minutes for the sauce
GRILLING TIME: 6–8 minutes

4 boneless, skinless chicken breasts, trimmed, 125–175 g/
4–6 oz each
3/4 teaspoon sea salt
1/2 teaspoon ground black pepper
8 whole sage leaves
8 thin slices Parma ham
Extra-virgin olive oil

SAUCE
40 g/1½ oz unsalted butter
1 small shallot, finely chopped
4 tablespoons dry white wine
250 ml/8 fl oz chicken stock
2 tablespoons fresh lemon juice
25 g/1 oz unsalted butter, cold
Sea salt
Ground black pepper

NOTE!

The ham and sage that you wrap around each chicken breast will
flavour the meat during grilling.

1 Prepare the grill for direct cooking over medium heat
(180–230°C/350–450°F).

2 One at a time, place each breast, smooth side down,
between two sheets of clingfilm and pound to an even
1-cm/1/2-inch thickness.

3 Season the chicken on both sides with the salt and pepper.
Place the chicken, smooth side down, on a work surface.
Lay 2 sage leaves on top of each piece of chicken. Then wrap
2 slices of Parma ham around each breast, staggering them
slightly so the meat is completely covered and the ends meet
on the other side. Press the ham so that it clings to the chicken.
Lightly brush both sides with oil.

4 In a frying pan over a medium-high heat, melt 40 g/1½ oz
butter. Add the shallot and cook for 3–4 minutes, until it
just turns tender, stirring occasionally. Add the wine and bring
to a simmer. Add the chicken stock and lemon juice. Bring to the
boil and reduce by half, about 10 minutes, stirring occasionally.
The sauce should barely coat the back of a spoon. Remove the
sauce from the heat and blend in the cold butter, half at a time.
Season with salt and pepper and set aside.

5 Brush the cooking grates clean. Grill the chicken, sage
side down, over **grilling/direct medium heat** for 3–4
minutes, with the lid closed as much as possible. Using a metal
spatula, gently turn the chicken over, taking care not to tear the
ham. Grill for 3–4 minutes more. To check for doneness, cut into
the underside of one breast. The meat should be opaque all the
way to the centre. Remove from the grill and allow to rest for
3–5 minutes. Warm the sauce over a medium heat.

6 Serve the chicken warm with the sauce.

SERVES: 4

PARMA HAM-WRAPPED CHICKEN

WITH FIG-BALSAMIC GLAZE

PREP TIME: 10 minutes, plus about 15 minutes for the glaze
GRILLING TIME: 6–8 minutes

GLAZE

4 tablespoons balsamic vinegar
2 dried figs, finely chopped
1 small shallot, finely chopped
1 tablespoon honey
1 tablespoon fresh lemon juice

4 boneless, skinless chicken breasts, 125–175 g/
    4–6 oz each
Sea salt
Ground black pepper
4 thin slices Parma ham
8 fresh figs, about 30 g/1¼ oz each, stalks removed, cut in
    half lengthways
Extra-virgin olive oil
200 g/7 oz baby rocket
50 g/2 oz Parmesan cheese, thinly shaved

1 In a small saucepan over a medium heat, combine the vinegar, dried figs and shallot. Bring to the boil, reduce the heat to low, and simmer for about 10 minutes, until almost all of the liquid has reduced to a thick, syrupy consistency. Remove from the heat and stir in the honey and lemon juice. Pour the glaze through a fine sieve into a glass or stainless-steel bowl, and discard the pulp. Set aside to cool.

2 One at a time, place each breast, smooth (skin) side down, between two sheets of clingfilm and pound to an even 1-cm/½-inch thickness. Season both sides of the chicken with salt and pepper. Wrap one piece of Parma ham around the centre of each breast, pressing the loose ends of the ham down so the meat stays together. Lightly brush the chicken on both sides and the cut sides of the figs with oil.

3 Prepare the grill for direct cooking over medium heat (180–230°C/350–450°F).

4 Brush the cooking grates clean. Grill the chicken, smooth (skin) side down first, over **grilling/direct medium heat** for 6–8 minutes, with the lid closed as much as possible, until the meat is firm to the touch and opaque all the way to the centre, turning once or twice. At the same time, grill the figs over **grilling/direct medium heat** for about 4 minutes, until well marked and heated through, turning once after 3 minutes.

5 Divide the rocket evenly among four plates. Place one chicken breast on each serving of rocket along with 4 fig halves. Drizzle the chicken and rocket with the glaze and top with the cheese.

SERVES: 4

NOTE!

The concentrated intensity of dried figs works best for the glaze here, but for grilling you will appreciate the plumpness and juiciness of fresh figs.

CHICKEN GYROS

WITH TOMATO TZATZIKI

PREP TIME: 30 minutes
MARINATING TIME: 30 minutes
GRILLING TIME: 8–10 minutes

SAUCE

250 g/8 oz Greek yogurt
2 tablespoons finely chopped mint
1 tablespoon extra-virgin olive oil
1½ teaspoons fresh lemon juice
½ teaspoon sea salt
¼ teaspoon ground black pepper
200 g/7 oz ripe tomatoes, finely chopped
75 g/3 oz cucumber, finely diced

MARINADE

3 tablespoons extra-virgin olive oil
3 tablespoons fresh lemon juice
1 tablespoon dried oregano
1 garlic clove, finely chopped
½ teaspoon sea salt
¼ teaspoon ground black pepper
pinch crushed chilli flakes

750 g/1½ lb chicken strips
1 small red onion, cut crossways into 1-cm/½-inch slices
Extra-virgin olive oil
6 flatbreads or pittas

1 In a glass or stainless-steel bowl, whisk the yogurt, mint, oil, lemon juice, salt and pepper. Add the tomato and cucumber and stir to combine.

2 In a large glass or stainless-steel bowl, whisk the marinade ingredients. Add the chicken to the bowl and turn to coat evenly. Marinate at room temperature for 30 minutes.

3 Prepare the grill for direct cooking over medium heat (180–230°C/350–450°F).

4 Lightly brush the onion slices on both sides with oil. Remove the chicken from the bowl, letting the herbs cling to the chicken. Discard the marinade. Brush the cooking grates clean. Grill the chicken and onion slices over **grilling/direct medium heat** for 6–8 minutes, with the lid closed as much as possible, until the meat is firm to the touch and the juices run clear and the onion is tender, turning once. Remove from the grill.

5 Warm the flat breads on the grill over **grilling/direct medium heat** for about 2 minutes, until lightly charred, turning once or twice.

6 Layer some chicken, sauce and onion inside the flat-breads and serve warm or at room temperature. Serving suggestion: Grilled Vegetable and Orzo Salad (for recipe, see page 139).

SERVES: 6

TURKISH CHICKEN KEBABS

WITH RED PEPPER AND WALNUT SAUCE

PREP TIME: 15 minutes
MARINATING TIME: up to 1 hour
GRILLING TIME: 8–10 minutes
SPECIAL EQUIPMENT: metal or bamboo skewers (if using bamboo, soak in water for at least 30 minutes)

1 teaspoon dry mustard
1 teaspoon garlic granules
1 teaspoon sea salt
$^1/_2$ teaspoon ground cumin
$^1/_2$ teaspoon ground black pepper
4 tablespoons extra-virgin olive oil
6 boneless, skinless chicken breasts, about 175 g/6 oz each

SAUCE

$1^1/_2$ roasted red peppers (from a jar), drained
50 g/2 oz toasted walnuts
125 ml/4 fl oz extra-virgin olive oil
4 tablespoons plain breadcrumbs
2 tablespoons balsamic vinegar
$^1/_2$ teaspoon ground cumin
$^1/_4$ teaspoon sea salt
$^1/_4$ teaspoon ground black pepper

1 In a large bowl mix the mustard, garlic granules, salt, cumin and pepper. Add the oil and stir to combine.

2 Cut each chicken breast in half lengthways and then cut each half crossways into 2.5–3.5 cm/1–1$^1/_2$-inch pieces. Place the chicken pieces in the bowl and turn to coat them evenly.

3 Skewer the chicken pieces so that the pieces are touching but not crammed together. Cover and refrigerate for up to 1 hour.

4 In the bowl of a food processor or blender, combine the sauce ingredients and process to create a pesto-like consistency. For a thinner sauce, add a bit of warm water.

5 Prepare the grill for direct cooking over medium heat (180–230°C/350–450°F).

6 Brush the cooking grates clean. Grill the kebabs over **grilling/direct medium heat** for 8–10 minutes, with the lid closed as much as possible, until the meat is firm to the touch and opaque all the way to the centre, turning once or twice. Remove from the grill and serve warm with the sauce.

SERVES: 6

CHICKEN CORDON BLEU PANINI

WITH HAM AND SWISS CHEESE

PREP TIME: 15 minutes
MARINATING TIME: 20–30 minutes
GRILLING TIME: 14–20 minutes
SPECIAL EQUIPMENT: roasting tray and 2 foil-wrapped bricks or
cast-iron frying pan

MARINADE

2 tablespoons extra-virgin olive oil
1 tablespoon Dijon mustard
1 teaspoon finely chopped garlic
½ teaspoon sea salt
¼ teaspoon ground black pepper

2 boneless, skinless chicken breasts, 175–250 g/6–8 oz each
Dijon mustard
8 slices crusty sourdough bread, each 1 cm/½ inch thick
8 thin slices deli ham, about 250 g/8 oz total
8 thin slices Emmental cheese, about 250 g/8 oz total
Extra-virgin olive oil

1 Prepare the grill for direct cooking over medium heat (180–230°C/350–450°F).

2 In a medium bowl whisk the marinade ingredients. Add the chicken to the bowl and turn to coat evenly. Allow the chicken to marinate at room temperature for 20–30 minutes.

3 Remove the chicken from the bowl and discard the marinade. Brush the cooking grates clean. Grill the chicken, smooth (skin) side down first, over **grilling/direct medium heat** for 8–12 minutes, with the lid closed as much as possible, until the meat is firm to the touch and opaque all the way to the centre, turning once or twice. Remove from the grill and allow to rest for 3–5 minutes. Cut the chicken into 1-cm/ ½-inch strips.

4 Reduce the temperature of the grill to low heat (180–230°C/350–450°F).

5 Lightly spread mustard on one side of 4 slices of bread. Top with 2 slices of ham and 2 slices of cheese. Layer each sandwich with chicken strips and top with the remaining bread slices. Lightly brush each sandwich on both sides with oil, and press down on each sandwich so it is compacted. Brush the cooking grates clean. Place the sandwiches over direct low heat and put a roasting tray with 2 foil-wrapped bricks (or use a cast-iron frying pan) directly on top of the sandwiches. Grill, uncovered, for 3–4 minutes. Carefully remove the weight, turn the sandwiches over, replace the weight, and grill for 3–4 minutes more, until the bread is toasted and the cheese has melted. Remove from the grill and serve right away.

SERVES: 4

CHICKEN SOUVLAKI

WITH MINTY FETA DRESSING

PREP TIME: 40 minutes
GRILLING TIME: 6–8 minutes
SPECIAL EQUIPMENT: 8 metal or bamboo skewers (if using bamboo, soak in water for at least 30 minutes)

MARINADE

15 g/1½ oz flat-leaf parsley, roughly chopped
4 tablespoons dry white wine
4 tablespoons extra-virgin olive oil
Grated zest and juice from ½ lemon
1 teaspoon garlic granules
1 teaspoon dried oregano
1 teaspoon paprika
¾ teaspoon sea salt
¼ teaspoon ground black pepper

4 boneless, skinless chicken breasts, about 175 g/6 oz each

SALAD

175 g/6 oz romaine lettuce leaves, roughly chopped
2 ripe tomatoes, cut into wedges
1 yellow or orange pepper, stalk removed, deseeded and cut
    into bite-sized pieces
½ cucumber, cut into 1-cm/½-inch chunks
75 g/3 oz pitted Kalamata olives
50 g/2 oz red onion, very thinly sliced

DRESSING

75 g/3 oz feta cheese, crumbled
4 tablespoons fresh mint leaves
2 tablespoons extra-virgin olive oil
1 tablespoon white wine vinegar
1 small garlic clove, roughly chopped

1 In a large glass or stainless-steel bowl, whisk the marinade ingredients. Cut the chicken lengthways into even strips, each about 2.5–3.5 cm/1–1½ inches thick. Cut the strips crossways into 2.5–3.5-cm/1–1½-inch pieces. Add the chicken to the bowl with the marinade and mix well. Cover and refrigerate until needed.

2 In a large bowl combine the salad ingredients. Cover and refrigerate until just before serving.

3 In a blender or food processor, combine the dressing ingredients, including 2 tablespoons of water. Blend until thick and smooth, scraping down the sides as needed. Season with salt and pepper.

4 Prepare the grill for direct cooking over high heat (230–290°C/450–550°F).

5 Thread the chicken pieces on to skewers. Discard any leftover marinade. Lightly coat the chicken pieces with oil.

6 Brush the cooking grates clean. Grill the skewers over **grilling/direct high heat** for 6–8 minutes, with the lid closed as much as possible, until the meat is firm to the touch and opaque all the way to the centre, turning once or twice.

7 Just before serving, add enough of the dressing to coat the salad ingredients lightly. Mix well.

8 Remove the chicken from the skewers while still warm and place on top of the salad. Season with salt and pepper. Serve any remaining dressing on the side.

SERVES: 4–6

DUCK BREASTS

WITH PRUNES, SHALLOTS AND ARMAGNAC

PREP TIME: 25 minutes
GRILLING TIME: 10–12 minutes

12 pitted prunes, about 125 g/4½ oz total, each cut in half
2 tablespoons Armagnac
1 tablespoon extra-virgin olive oil
2 shallots, finely chopped
250 ml/8 fl oz port
125 g/4 fl oz chicken stock
2 tablespoons balsamic vinegar
2 large sprigs fresh thyme
½ teaspoon ground coriander
Coarse salt
Freshly ground black pepper
4 boneless duck breasts (with skin), each 200–250 g/7–8 oz,
    trimmed of excess fat, patted dry

1 In a small bowl combine the prunes and Armagnac. Allow to stand for 15 minutes.

2 In a saucepan over a medium heat, warm the oil. Add the shallot and sauté for about 3 minutes, until slightly softened. Add the prunes and Armagnac, the port, chicken stock, vinegar, thyme sprigs and coriander. Bring to the boil, and then reduce the heat to medium-low. Simmer, uncovered for 10–12 minutes, until the liquid is reduced by about half and the sauce is thickened, stirring occasionally to break up the prunes. Discard the thyme sprigs. Season with ½ teaspoon salt and ½ teaspoon pepper. Cover to keep warm.

3 Prepare the grill for direct cooking over medium-high heat (200–230°C/400–450°F).

4 Score the skin of each duck breast on the diagonal in a crisscross pattern (do not cut through the breast meat) and season evenly with ¾ teaspoon salt and ¾ teaspoon pepper.

5 Grill the duck breasts, skin side down first, over **grilling/ direct medium-high heat**, with the lid closed, until cooked to your desired doneness, 10–12 minutes for medium rare, turning once (if flare-ups occur, move the duck temporarily over indirect heat). Remove from the grill and allow to rest for 3–5 minutes.

6 Rewarm the sauce over low heat, if necessary. Cut the duck crossways into 7-mm/⅓-inch slices and serve warm with the sauce spooned on top.

SERVES: 4

123

PASTA AND RISOTTO

LEMON RISOTTO

WITH GRILLED ASPARAGUS

PREP TIME: 10 minutes, plus about 30 minutes for the risotto
GRILLING TIME: 6–8 minutes

500 g/1 lb asparagus, no more than 1 cm/¹⁄₂ inch wide at the base, tough ends removed
Extra-virgin olive oil
Coarse salt
1.5 litres/2¹⁄₂ pints chicken stock
1 onion, finely chopped
300 g/10 oz arborio rice
¹⁄₂ cup dry white wine
50 g/2 oz Parmesan cheese, finely grated, plus extra for garnish
2 teaspoons finely grated lemon zest
2 tablespoons fresh lemon juice
15 g/¹⁄₂ oz unsalted butter
¹⁄₄ teaspoon freshly ground black pepper
1 tablespoon finely chopped fresh tarragon or mint

1 Prepare the grill for direct cooking over medium heat (180–230°C/350–450°F).

2 Drizzle the asparagus with oil, lightly season with salt, and then grill over **grilling/direct medium heat** for 6–8 minutes, with the lid closed, until browned in spots and crisp-tender, turning occasionally. Remove from the grill, cut off the tips, and cut the stalks into 1-cm/¹⁄₂-inch pieces. Reserve eight of the asparagus tips for garnish.

3 In a saucepan over a high heat, bring the chicken stock to a simmer. Keep warm.

4 In a large saucepan over a medium heat, warm 1 tablespoon oil. Add the onion and ¹⁄₂ teaspoon salt and sauté for 3–4 minutes, until softened but not browned. Add the rice and cook until the grains are coated with the oil and turn opaque, about 2 minutes, stirring frequently. Add the wine and stir for about 1 minute, until evaporated. Add 250 ml/8 fl oz of the warm stock. Simmer until the rice has absorbed nearly all of the liquid, stirring occasionally. Add the remaining stock 125 ml/4 fl oz at a time, stirring until nearly all of the liquid is absorbed before adding the next addition, 20–25 minutes in all. At this point the risotto should be creamy and the grains should be plump and tender, yet firm to the bite.

5 Remove from the heat. Stir in the cheese, lemon zest and juice, butter, ¹⁄₂ teaspoon salt and pepper. Fold in the asparagus and tarragon. Divide among serving bowls. Garnish with the reserved asparagus tips and the additional cheese. Serve immediately.

SERVES: 4

RISOTTO

WITH GRILLED WILD MUSHROOMS AND FRESH HERBS

PREP TIME: 10 minutes, plus about 30 minutes for the risotto
GRILLING TIME: 6–8 minutes
SPECIAL EQUIPMENT: perforated grill pan

500 g/1 lb mixed wild mushrooms, such as chanterelle, cremini
    and porcini, cut into 5-mm/¼-inch slices
Coarse salt
1.5 litres/2½ pints chicken stock
1 tablespoon extra-virgin olive oil
2 shallots, finely chopped
300 g/10 oz arborio rice
125 ml/4 fl oz dry white wine
¼ teaspoon freshly ground black pepper
50 g/2 oz Parmesan cheese, finely grated
15 g/½ oz unsalted butter
2 tablespoons finely chopped chives
2 tablespoons finely chopped flat-leaf parsley
2 teaspoons finely chopped thyme leaves

1 Prepare the grill for direct cooking over medium heat (180–230°C/350–450°F) and preheat a perforated grill pan.

2 Spread the mushrooms in a single layer on the grill pan and season with ½ teaspoon salt. Grill over **grilling/ direct medium heat** for 6–8 minutes, with the lid closed, until golden brown and tender, turning once or twice. Transfer to a plate.

3 In a saucepan over a high heat, bring the chicken stock to a simmer. Keep warm.

4 In a large saucepan over a medium heat, warm the oil. Add the shallots and sauté for about 3 minutes, until softened but not browned. Add the rice and cook until the grains are coated with the oil and turn opaque, about 2 minutes, stirring frequently. Add the wine and stir for about 1 minute, until evaporated. Add 250 ml/8 fl oz of the warm stock. Simmer until the rice has absorbed nearly all of the liquid, stirring occasionally. Add the remaining stock 125 ml/4 fl oz at a time, stirring until nearly all of the liquid is absorbed before adding the next addition, 20 to 25 minutes in all. At this point the risotto should be creamy and the grains should be plump and tender, yet firm to the bite.

5 Remove from the heat. Stir in 1 teaspoon salt, the pepper, cheese, butter, chives, parsley and thyme. Fold in the mushrooms. Divide among bowls and serve immediately.

SERVES: 4–6

LASAGNE

WITH GRILLED AUBERGINE, PEPPERS AND COURGETTES

PREP TIME: 20 minutes, plus 25 minutes for the sauce
GRILLING TIME: 1–1¼ hours
SPECIAL EQUIPMENT: 25 x 20-cm/10 x 8-inch grill-proof baking dish

SAUCE

1 tablespoon extra-virgin olive oil
2 onions, finely chopped
2 garlic cloves, finely chopped
¼ teaspoon crushed chilli flakes, or to taste
2 cans (each 400 g/13 oz) chopped Italian plum tomatoes in juice
½ teaspoon dried oregano

Coarse salt
Freshly ground black pepper
1 large red pepper
1 aubergine, about 500 g/1 lb, cut lengthways into 1-cm/½-inch
  slices
2 courgettes, each about 175 g/6 oz, cut lengthways into 1-cm/
  ½-inch slices
Extra-virgin olive oil
500 g/1 lb full-fat ricotta cheese
1 large egg
150 g/5 oz pecorino cheese, finely grated
250 g/8 oz fresh mozzarella cheese, torn into small pieces
250 g/8 oz dried lasagne sheets

1 In a large saucepan over a medium heat, warm the oil. Add the onion and sauté for about 3 minutes, until softened. Add the garlic and chilli flakes and sauté for about 1 minute, until fragrant. Add the tomatoes, oregano, 1 teaspoon salt and ¼ teaspoon pepper and simmer over a medium-low heat for about 20 minutes, until slightly thickened, stirring occasionally. Remove from the heat.

2 Prepare the grill for direct and indirect cooking over medium heat (180–230°C/350–450°F).

3 Grill the pepper over **grilling/direct medium heat** for 10–12 minutes, with the lid closed, until blackened and blistered all over, turning occasionally. Put the pepper in a bowl and cover with clingfilm to trap the steam. Allow to stand for about 10 minutes, and then remove from the bowl and peel away and discard the charred skin. Cut off and discard the stalk and seeds, and then cut the pepper into 2.5-cm/1-inch strips.

4 Generously brush the aubergine on both sides with oil. Lightly brush the courgette with oil. Season the aubergine and courgette with salt and pepper. Grill the vegetables over **grilling/direct medium heat,** with the lid closed, until nicely marked and tender on both sides, 8–10 minutes for the aubergine and 4–6 minutes for the courgette, turning once or twice.

5 Whisk the ricotta, egg, 50 g/2 oz of the pecorino, 1 teaspoon salt and ½ teaspoon pepper until smooth.

6 Spoon 125 ml/4 fl oz of the sauce into the bottom of an 25 x 20-cm/10 x 8-inch grill-proof baking dish. Place a layer of pasta sheets over the sauce, breaking to fit as necessary. Spread about 125 ml/4 fl oz ricotta mixture over the pasta sheets. Arrange the aubergine slices over the ricotta. Drizzle about 125 ml/4 fl oz sauce over the aubergine. Scatter one-third of the remaining pecorino and one-third of the mozzarella over the sauce. Top with another layer of pasta sheets and repeat the layering process with 125 ml/4 fl oz sauce, 125 ml/4 fl oz ricotta mixture, the courgettes and red peppers, 125 ml/4 fl oz sauce, half of the remaining pecorino and half of the remaining mozzarella. Top with the last layer of pasta sheets. Spread with the remaining ricotta. Drizzle spoonfuls of the sauce over the ricotta. Top with the remaining pecorino and mozzarella.

7 Cook the lasagne over **roasting/indirect medium heat** (keep the temperature of the grill as close to 180°C/350°F as possible) for 45–50 minutes, with the lid closed, until thoroughly cooked and the cheese is melted and bubbly. If the top begins to brown before the lasagne is thoroughly cooked, loosely cover with foil. Allow the lasagne to cool for 10 minutes before cutting and serving.

SERVES: 8

131

ORECCHIETTE

WITH ROASTED CAULIFLOWER, CRISPY PARMA HAM AND PEAS

PREP TIME: 25 minutes
GRILLING TIME: about 14 minutes
SPECIAL EQUIPMENT: perforated grill pan

75 g/3 oz thinly sliced Parma ham
1 medium head cauliflower, broken into large florets and cut
lengthways into 5-mm/¼-inch slices
Extra-virgin olive oil
Coarse salt
½ teaspoon crushed chilli flakes
500 g/1 lb dried orecchiette
225 g/7½ oz frozen peas, defrosted, at room temperature
½ teaspoon freshly ground black pepper
100 g/3½ oz Parmesan cheese, finely grated, plus extra for
garnish
Zest of 1 lemon

1 Prepare the grill for indirect cooking over medium heat
(as close to 200°C/400°F as possible) and preheat a
perforated grill pan over indirect heat for about 10 minutes.

2 Arrange the Parma ham in a single layer, without
overlapping, on the grill pan. Cook over **roasting/indirect
medium heat** for about 4 minutes, with the lid closed, until
slightly shrivelled and dry. Remove from the grill and, when
cool enough to handle, break into shards.

3 In a bowl combine the cauliflower, 1 tablespoon oil,
½ teaspoon salt and the chilli flakes and stir to coat.
Spread in a single layer on the grill pan and grill over **roasting/
indirect medium heat** for about 10 minutes, with the lid closed,
until tender and golden brown in spots, stirring once or twice
after the undersides brown.

4 Bring a large saucepan of salted water to a rolling
boil, and cook the pasta until al dente. Drain, reserving
250 ml/8 fl oz pasta water. In a large serving bowl combine the
pasta, 2 tablespoons oil, the peas, pepper, ½ teaspoon salt and
some of the reserved pasta water, if needed. Toss to combine.
Fold in the cauliflower, ham and cheese. Serve immediately,
garnished with additional cheese and lemon zest.

SERVES: 4–6

PAELLA

WITH CHORIZO, CHICKEN AND PRAWNS

PREP TIME: 20 minutes
GRILLING TIME: about 30 minutes
SPECIAL EQUIPMENT: paella pan or 35-cm/14-inch cast-iron
frying pan

Extra-virgin olive oil
1 teaspoon Spanish paprika
Coarse salt
Freshly ground black pepper
500 g/1 lb boneless, skinless chicken thighs, cut into
    3.5-cm/1½-inch pieces
⅛ teaspoon ground cayenne pepper
18 raw tiger prawns
1 litre/1¾ pints chicken stock
½ teaspoon saffron threads
375 g/12 oz cured Spanish chorizo sausage, cut crossways into
    1-cm/½-inch slices
2 onions, finely chopped
4 garlic cloves, finely chopped
1 can (400 g/13 oz) whole Italian plum tomatoes in juice, drained
    and hand crushed
1 teaspoon smoked paprika
400 g/13 oz Spanish or Valencia rice

1 In a bowl whisk 1 tablespoon oil, the Spanish paprika, ½ teaspoon salt and ¼ teaspoon pepper. Add the chicken pieces and stir to coat.

2 In another bowl whisk 1 tablespoon oil, ½ teaspoon salt and the cayenne pepper. Add the prawns and stir to coat.

3 Prepare the grill for direct cooking over medium heat (180–230°C/350–450°F) and preheat a paella pan for about 10 minutes.

4 In a saucepan over a medium heat, warm the stock until it reaches a simmer. Add the saffron, and then turn off the heat.

5 Add 1 tablespoon oil to a paella pan, and then add the chorizo. Cook over **grilling/direct medium heat** for about 3 minutes, with the lid closed, until golden brown on both sides, turning once. Using a slotted spoon, transfer the sausage to a bowl. There should be rendered fat from the chorizo remaining in the pan. If not, add 1 tablespoon oil. Arrange the chicken in one layer in the paella pan. Cook over **grilling/direct medium heat** for 4–6 minutes, with the lid closed, until golden brown on both sides, turning once. Using a slotted spoon, transfer the chicken to the bowl with the chorizo.

6 Add the onion to the paella pan and sauté over **grilling/ direct medium heat** for about 3 minutes, with the lid closed, until softened without colouring, stirring once. Add the garlic and cook until fragrant, about 30 seconds, stirring constantly. Add the tomatoes and smoked paprika and stir to combine, and then add the rice and 1 teaspoon salt and stir to coat. Pour the stock over the rice and smooth the rice in an even layer. Do not stir the rice after this point. Place the chorizo and chicken over the rice and drizzle with any accumulated juices. Cook the paella over **grilling/direct medium heat** for 12–15 minutes, with the lid closed, until most of the liquid has been absorbed, rotating the pan once or twice to ensure even cooking.

7 Nestle the prawns into the rice and continue cooking for about 5 minutes, until the prawns are firm to the touch and opaque in the centre and the rice is al dente. Remove the pan from the grill. Cover with foil and allow to stand for 10 minutes. Serve immediately.

SERVES: 6

NOTE!

Do not stir the rice once it's in the pan. This will help to create a golden crust on the bottom, called the socarrat, which is considered a delicacy. Towards the end of cooking, you might hear the rice crackling, which is the sound of the crust forming. If you don't have a paella pan, a large cast-iron frying pan is a good substitute, preferably 35 cm/ 14 inches in diameter so the rice may be spread in a thin layer.

UMBRIAN-STYLE PORK RAGU

WITH PAPPARDELLE

PREP TIME: 25 minutes
GRILLING TIME: 2½–3 hours
SPECIAL EQUIPMENT: grill-proof cast-iron casserole

1 piece of boneless pork shoulder, about 1 kg/2 lb trimmed of excess fat
Extra-virgin olive oil
Coarse salt
Freshly ground black pepper
150 g/5 oz carrots, diced
100 g/3½ oz celery, diced
2 onions, finely chopped
4 garlic cloves, finely chopped
1 teaspoon dried thyme
1 teaspoon dried oregano
½ teaspoon crushed chilli flakes
250 ml/8 fl oz full-bodied red wine
2 cans (400 g/13 oz) chopped Italian plum tomatoes in juice
250 ml/8 fl oz chicken stock, plus more as needed
500 g/1 lb dried pappardelle
50 g/2 oz pecorino cheese, finely grated

1 Prepare the grill for direct and indirect cooking over medium heat (180–230°C/350–450°F) and preheat a cast-iron casserole, without its lid, over indirect heat.

2 Lightly coat the pork with oil and season evenly with ¾ teaspoon salt and ½ teaspoon pepper. Grill the pork on the cooking grates over **grilling/direct medium heat** for about 10 minutes, with the lid closed, until browned on all sides, turning occasionally. Remove from the grill.

3 Slide the casserole over **grilling/direct medium heat** and add 1 tablespoon oil, the carrots, celery and onion. Close the lid and cook for 6–8 minutes, until the vegetables are slightly softened, stirring frequently. Add the garlic, thyme, oregano and chilli flakes and cook until fragrant, about 1 minute, stirring constantly. Add the wine and bring to the boil, and then stir in the tomatoes and 250 ml/8 fl oz stock. Transfer the pork and any accumulated juices to the casserole and turn to coat. Cover the pot and slide over **roasting/indirect low heat**, reducing the heat to maintain a temperature as close to 150°C/300°F as possible. Cook for 2¼–2½ hours, with the grill lid closed, until the pork is fork tender, turning the pork once every hour and adding more stock 125 ml/4 fl oz at a time if the pan juices reduce too much and the mixture is dry.

4 Remove the pork from the casserole and keep the pot on the grill. Shred the pork, discarding any fat or gristle. Return the meat to the casserole and add ¾ teaspoon salt and ¾ teaspoon pepper. If necessary, cook, with the casserole uncovered and the grill lid closed, until the sauce is slightly thickened, 2–3 minutes. If the sauce is already thickened, this will not be necessary.

5 Bring a large saucepan of salted water to a rolling boil. Cook the pappardelle until al dente; drain. Divide the pasta among serving plates and spoon the ragu over the top. Serve immediately and garnish with cheese.

SERVES: 4–6

PRAWN FRA DIAVOLO 〰

WITH LINGUINE

PREP TIME: 20 minutes, plus about 25 minutes for the sauce
GRILLING TIME: 2–4 minutes
SPECIAL EQUIPMENT: stick blender (optional)

3 tablespoons extra-virgin olive oil
1 garlic clove, finely chopped
1½ teaspoons crushed chilli flakes
2 cans (each 400 g/13 oz) whole Italian plum tomatoes in juice
125 ml/4 fl oz dry white wine
1 teaspoon dried oregano
1½ teaspoons coarse salt
½ teaspoon freshly ground black pepper
750 g/1½ lb raw tiger prawns, peeled and deveined
500 g/1 lb dried linguine
4 tablespoons chopped flat-leaf parsley

1 In a large frying pan over a medium heat, warm 1 tablespoon of the oil. Add the garlic and 1 teaspoon of the chilli flakes and cook until fragrant, about 1 minute, stirring constantly. Add the tomatoes, wine, oregano, 1 teaspoon of the salt and the pepper. Bring to the boil, and then simmer for 20–25 minutes, uncovered, until the sauce thickens, stirring occasionally. If liked, blend with a stick blender until the tomatoes are broken up into small pieces. Remove from the heat and keep warm.

2 Prepare the grill for direct cooking over high heat (230–290°C/450–550°F).

3 In a large bowl whisk the remaining 2 tablespoons oil, ½ teaspoon salt and ½ teaspoon chilli flakes. Add the prawns and gently stir to coat.

4 Grill the prawns over **grilling/direct high heat** for 2–4 minutes, with the lid closed, until firm to the touch and just turning opaque in the centre, turning once. Remove from the heat.

5 Bring a large saucepan of salted water to a rolling boil. Add the linguine and cook until al dente. Drain the pasta and add it to the frying pan with the sauce, and then add the grilled prawns and half the parsley and toss to combine. Garnish with the remaining parsley and serve immediately.

SERVES: 4

SPAGHETTI À LA PUTTANESCA

WITH GRILL-ROASTED TOMATO SAUCE

PREP TIME: 15 minutes
GRILLING TIME: 11–18 minutes
SPECIAL EQUIPMENT: large, grill-proof frying pan

4 tablespoons extra-virgin olive oil
4 garlic cloves, finely chopped
½ teaspoon crushed chilli flakes
4 anchovy fillets, rinsed, patted dry, chopped
750 g/1½ lb grape or cherry tomatoes, each cut in half
125 g/4 oz oil-cured black olives, coarsely chopped
2 tablespoons capers, rinsed and drained
½ teaspoon dried oregano
1 teaspoon granulated sugar
½ teaspoon coarse salt, or to taste (optional)
500 g/1 lb dried spaghetti
2 tablespoons finely chopped flat-leaf parsley

1 Prepare the grill for direct and indirect cooking over medium heat (as close to 200°C/400°F as possible).

2 In a large, grill-proof frying pan over **grilling/direct medium heat**, warm the oil. Add the garlic and chilli flakes and sauté until fragrant, about 1 minute. Add the anchovies and sauté for 1–2 minutes, until they begin to dissolve. Add the tomatoes and cook for 6–10 minutes, until they soften and collapse, stirring frequently. Keep the grill lid closed as much as possible during grilling. Slide the frying pan over **roasting/indirect medium heat**. Stir in the olives, capers, oregano and sugar and continue cooking for 3–5 minutes, with the lid closed, until the sauce is thickened, stirring occasionally. Taste the sauce and add the salt, if liked.

3 Meanwhile, bring a large saucepan of salted water to a rolling boil. Once you've added the last ingredients to the sauce, add the spaghetti to the boiling water and cook until al dente. Drain. Put the pasta back in the pan and pour most of the sauce over the pasta. Gently toss with tongs. Divide the pasta among four bowls, top with additional sauce, and garnish with parsley.

SERVES: 4

NOTE!

The salt from the anchovies and olives may provide all the salt you need for the sauce, so taste for seasoning before adding any additional salt.

GRILLED VEGETABLE

AND ORZO SALAD

PREP TIME: 20 minutes, plus about 10 minutes for the orzo
GRILLING TIME: 12–15 minutes

250 g/8 oz orzo pasta
6 tablespoons extra-virgin olive oil
2 tablespoons balsamic vinegar
2 teaspoons garlic, finely chopped
2 teaspoons Dijon mustard
Sea salt
Ground black pepper
2 corn on the cobs, husked
2 medium courgettes, halved lengthways
1 bell pepper, quartered and deseeded
250 g/8 oz small cherry tomatoes
125 g/4 oz feta cheese, crumbled
4 tablespoons roughly chopped flat-leaf parsley or basil

1 Prepare the grill for direct cooking over medium heat (180–230°C/350–450°F).

2 Cook the orzo according to package directions. Drain and set aside in a large glass or stainless-steel bowl.

3 In a small glass or stainless-steel bowl, whisk the oil, vinegar, garlic, mustard, 1 teaspoon salt and 1 teaspoon pepper until smooth. Lightly coat the corn, courgettes and pepper with about half of the olive oil mixture. Reserve the remaining half for dressing the salad.

4 Brush the cooking grates clean. Grill the vegetables over **grilling/direct medium heat**, with the lid closed as much as possible, until lightly charred and crisp-tender, turning as needed. The corn will take 12–15 minutes and the courgettes and pepper will take 4–6 minutes. Remove the vegetables from the grill as they are done. Set aside to cool.

5 Cut the kernels off the cobs into the bowl of orzo. Use the back of a knife to scrape the juice from the cobs. Scrape off and discard any burnt pieces from the pepper quarters, and then cut the pepper and courgettes crossways into 1-cm/½-inch pieces. Add them to the bowl. Cut each tomato in half or into quarters, and add to the bowl along with the cheese and fresh herbs. Add as much of the remaining dressing as you like (you may not need all of it) and toss to coat. Season with salt and pepper. Serve at room temperature.

SERVES: 8

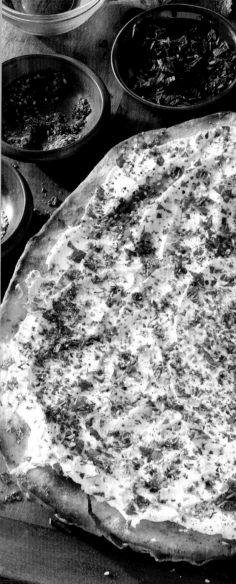

FLATBREADS AND PIZZA

PIZZA DOUGH

MAKES: 750 g/1½ lb, enough for two 30-cm/12-inch pizzas or flatbreads
PREP TIME: 15 minutes
RISING TIME: 1¼–1½ hours

250 ml/8 fl oz warm water (40–46°C/105–115°F)
1 tablespoon extra-virgin olive oil, plus more for the bowl
1¾ teaspoons sea salt
1½ teaspoons fast-action yeast
375 g/12 oz plain flour, plus more as needed

1a. Hand Method: In a large bowl combine the water, 1 tablespoon oil, salt and yeast. Stir in about 375 g/11 oz flour to make a stiff dough that cannot be stirred. Turn the dough out on to a floured work surface and knead by hand for about 6 minutes, working in the remaining flour, or more as needed, until the dough is smooth, supple and slightly tacky.

1b. Electric Stand Mixer Method: In the bowl of a stand mixer combine the water, 1 tablespoon oil, salt and yeast. Fit the mixer with the paddle attachment. Mix on low speed, adding enough of the flour to make a soft, slightly tacky dough that cleans the bowl. Switch to the dough hook and knead on medium speed for about 6 minutes, until the dough is smooth, supple, and slightly tacky.

1c. Food Processor Method: In a food processor fitted with a plastic dough blade, add 375 g/12 oz cups flour, the salt and yeast, and then pulse a few times to blend. Add 1 tablespoon oil to the water. With the motor running, pour the liquid through the feed tube to make a ball of dough that is soft, but not sticky, and rides on the top of the blade (there will be some shaggy crumbles of dough, too). If the dough is too moist, dust with 1 tablespoon flour; if the dough is too dry, sprinkle with 1 tablespoon water. Process briefly, check the dough again, and repeat until the dough is smooth and elastic. Process the dough for 30 seconds more.

2 Coat a medium bowl with oil. Shape the dough into a ball, place in the bowl, and turn to coat with the oil. Cover the bowl tightly with clingfilm. Allow to stand in a warm, draught-free area until the dough is doubled in volume, 1¼–1½ hours; or refrigerate the dough for 6–8 hours. Return to room temperature before using.

Whether you knead the dough by hand or process it using a food processor or stand mixer, it should look like this: smooth and supple.

GRILLED GARLIC BREAD

PREP TIME: 10 minutes
GRILLING TIME: about 10 minutes

BUTTER
125 g/4 oz unsalted butter, softened
1 tablespoon finely chopped garlic
½ teaspoon sea salt
½ teaspoon paprika

1 loaf Italian or French bread, cut in half lengthways
1 tablespoon finely chopped flat-leaf parsley

1 Prepare the grill for direct cooking over medium heat (180–230°C/350–450°F).

2 In a bowl mix the butter ingredients until evenly incorporated.

3 Spread the butter evenly over the cut sides of the bread. Grill the bread, cut sides down, over **grilling/ direct medium heat** for 1–2 minutes, with the lid open, until toasted. Remove from the grill and cut the bread into pieces, each about 5 cm/2 inches thick. Sprinkle parsley over the bread just before serving.

SERVES: 6–8

HERBED FLATBREADS

WITH LABNEH

PREP TIME: 15 minutes
GRILLING TIME: 12–14 minutes
SPECIAL EQUIPMENT: pizza stone, pizza peel (optional), silicone
    pastry brush

750 g/1½ lb Pizza Dough (for recipe, see page 142)
Plain flour
3 tablespoons extra-virgin olive oil
1 teaspoon coarse salt
250 g/8 oz labneh (Middle Eastern yogurt cheese)
2 teaspoons sesame seeds, toasted
1 teaspoon za'atar
½ teaspoon freshly ground black pepper
4 tablespoons roughly chopped mint

1 Prepare the grill for direct cooking over medium heat (180–230°C/350–450°F) and preheat a pizza stone for 15 minutes, following manufacturer's instructions.

2 Divide the dough into two equal balls. On a lightly floured work surface, using a rolling pin or your hands, roll or stretch out one ball of dough into a 30-cm/12-inch round. Lightly dust a pizza peel or a rimless baking sheet with flour. Transfer the dough round to the pizza peel. Brush the top of the dough with 1½ teaspoons of the oil. Slide on to the preheated pizza stone. Cook over **grilling/direct medium heat** for about 3 minutes, with the lid closed, until the underside is light brown and firm. Using the pizza peel, slide the dough off the pizza stone. Flip and brush the grilled side with 1 tablespoon of the oil, and season evenly with ½ teaspoon of the salt. Slide back on to the pizza stone and continue grilling over **grilling/direct medium heat** for 3–4 minutes more, with the lid closed, until the crust is golden brown.

3 Transfer to a chopping board. Immediately spread with half of the labneh, leaving a 5-mm/¼-inch border, and season with 1 teaspoon of the sesame seeds, ½ teaspoon of the za'atar, and ¼ teaspoon of the pepper. Scatter with 2 tablespoons of the mint. Cut into wedges and serve warm.

4 Use a silicone pastry brush to brush off any flour left on the pizza stone. Make another flatbread with the remaining ingredients.

MAKES: two 30-cm/12-inch flatbreads

NOTE!

Labneh is a fresh cheese sold in many Middle Eastern shops and some supermarkets. The consistency lies somewhere between crème fraîche and cream cheese. If unavailable, substitute a tangy, full-fat milk ricotta; or, stir 4 tablespoons of crème fraîche or softened goats' cheese into 175 g/6 oz of cream cheese. You can also make labneh at home: overnight, in the refrigerator, strain about 300 g/10 oz of full-fat Greek yogurt through a fine-mesh sieve.

ROSEMARY AND SEA SALT FLATBREADS

PREP TIME: 15 minutes
GRILLING TIME: 12–14 minutes
SPECIAL EQUIPMENT: pizza stone, pizza peel (optional), silicone pastry brush

750 g/1½ lb Pizza Dough (for recipe, see page 142)
Plain flour
3 tablespoons extra-virgin olive oil, plus more for serving
1½ teaspoons coarse sea salt
1 tablespoon finely chopped rosemary leaves
¼ teaspoon freshly ground black pepper

1 Prepare the grill for direct cooking over medium heat (180–230°C/350–450°F) and preheat a pizza stone for about 15 minutes, following manufacturer's instructions.

2 Divide the dough into two equal balls. On a lightly floured work surface, using a rolling pin or your hands, roll or stretch out one ball of dough into a 30-cm/12-inch round. Lightly dust a pizza peel or a rimless baking sheet with flour. Transfer the dough round to the pizza peel. Brush the top of the dough with 1½ teaspoons of the oil. Slide on to the preheated pizza stone. Cook over **grilling/direct medium heat** for about 3 minutes, with the lid closed, until the underside is light brown and firm.

3 Using the pizza peel, slide the dough off the pizza stone. Flip and brush the grilled side with 1 tablespoon of the oil and season evenly with ¾ teaspoon of the salt and 1½ teaspoons of the rosemary. Slide back on to the pizza stone and continue grilling over **grilling/direct medium heat** for 3–4 minutes more, with the lid closed, until the crust is golden brown.

4 Transfer the flatbread to a chopping board, drizzle with a little more oil, and season with ⅛ teaspoon of the pepper. Cut into wedges or slabs and serve warm.

5 Use a silicone pastry brush to brush off any flour left on the pizza stone. Make another flatbread with the remaining ingredients.

MAKES: two 30-cm/12-inch flatbreads

One simple way to move dough to the grill while keeping its nice round shape is to drape it over a rolling pin and hold it in place.

SWEET ONION AND ANCHOVY FLATBREADS

PREP TIME: 35 minutes
GRILLING TIME: 12–14 minutes
SPECIAL EQUIPMENT: pizza stone, pizza peel (optional), silicone pastry brush

750 g/1½ lb Pizza Dough (for recipe, see page 142)
3½ tablespoons extra-virgin olive oil
2 Spanish onions, each 300–375 g/10–12 oz, cut lengthways and then cut crossways into very thin slices
Coarse salt
2 large garlic cloves, finely chopped
1 tablespoon finely chopped rosemary leaves
Plain flour
24 oil-packed, cured anchovy fillets
Freshly ground black pepper

1 In a large nonstick frying pan over a medium heat, warm 2½ tablespoons of the oil. Add the onions and ½ teaspoon salt. Sauté for 15–20 minutes, until the onions are very soft and light golden, stirring frequently. If necessary, reduce the heat to medium-low to prevent the onions from scorching. Stir in the garlic and rosemary and cook for 1 minute more. Remove from the heat.

2 Prepare the grill for direct cooking over medium heat (180–230°C/350–450°F) and preheat a pizza stone for about 15 minutes, following manufacturer's instructions.

3 Divide the dough into two equal balls. On a lightly floured work surface, using a rolling pin or your hands, roll or stretch out one ball of dough into a 30-cm/12-inch round. Lightly dust a pizza peel or a rimless baking sheet with flour. Transfer the dough round to the pizza peel. Brush the top of the dough with 1½ teaspoons of the oil. Slide on to the preheated pizza stone. Cook over **grilling/direct medium heat** for about 3 minutes, with the lid closed, until the underside is light brown and firm.

4 Using the pizza peel, slide the dough off the pizza stone. Flip and evenly spread the grilled side with half of the onion mixture and half of the anchovies, leaving a 2.5-cm/1-inch border. Slide back on to the pizza stone and continue cooking over **grilling/direct medium heat** for 3–4 minutes more, with the lid closed, until the crust is golden brown. Transfer to a chopping board and season generously with pepper. Cut into wedges and serve warm.

5 Use a silicone pastry brush to brush off any flour left on the pizza stone. Make another flatbread with the remaining ingredients.

MAKES: two 30-cm/12-inch flatbreads

FLATBREADS

WITH BROCCOLI, RED PEPPERS AND ROASTED GARLIC

PREP TIME: 25 minutes
GRILLING TIME: about 1¼ hours
SPECIAL EQUIPMENT: perforated grill pan, pizza stone, pizza peel
(optional), silicone pastry brush

750 g/1½ lb Pizza Dough (for recipe, see page 142)
1 large head garlic
Extra-virgin olive oil
¼ teaspoon crushed chilli flakes
Coarse salt
Freshly ground black pepper
500 g/1 lb tenderstem broccoli or broccolini, 3 cm/2 inches
    trimmed from the thick stem ends
1 red pepper, 200–250 g/7–8 oz
Plain flour
250 g/8 oz fresh mozzarella cheese, drained and patted dry,
    thinly sliced
75 g/3 oz pecorino cheese, finely grated

1 Prepare the grill for direct and indirect cooking over medium-high heat (200–230°C/400–450°F).

2 Cut off the top of the head of garlic to expose the cloves, drizzle generously with oil, and then wrap in foil. Cook over **roasting/indirect medium-high heat** for 45–50 minutes, with the lid closed, until soft. Remove from the grill, carefully unwrap the foil to allow the steam to escape, and allow to cool. Squeeze the cloves into a small bowl. Add 2 tablespoons oil, the chilli flakes, and ⅛ teaspoon salt. Mash with a fork to form a paste.

3 Preheat a perforated grill pan over direct heat for 10 minutes. Whisk 1 tablespoon oil, ½ teaspoon salt and ¼ teaspoon pepper; add the broccoli and turn to coat. Arrange the broccoli in a single layer on the grill pan and cook over **grilling/direct medium-high heat** for 3–5 minutes depending on the thickness of the stalks, with the lid closed, until charred in spots and crisp-tender, turning occasionally. Transfer the broccoli to a bowl, and remove the grill pan from the grill.

4 Grill the pepper over **grilling/direct medium-high heat** for 10–12 minutes, with the lid closed, until blackened and blistered all over, turning occasionally. Put the pepper in a bowl and cover with clingfilm to trap the steam. Allow to stand for about 10 minutes. Remove and discard the charred skin, stalk and seeds and cut the pepper into 5-mm/¼-inch strips.

5 Preheat a pizza stone over direct heat for about 15 minutes, following manufacturer's instructions.

6 Divide the dough into two equal balls. On a lightly floured work surface, using a rolling pin or your hands, roll or stretch out one ball of dough into a 30-cm/12-inch round. Lightly dust a pizza peel or a rimless baking sheet with flour. Transfer the dough round to the pizza peel. Slide on to the preheated pizza stone. Cook over **grilling/direct medium-high heat** for about 3 minutes, with the lid closed, until the dough is golden brown and firm on the underside.

7 Using the pizza peel, slide the dough off the pizza stone. Flip and spread the grilled side with half of the roasted garlic mixture, leaving a 2.5-cm/1-inch border. Top with half of the mozzarella slices, half of the broccoli, half of the pepper, and half of the pecorino. Slide back on to the pizza stone and continue grilling over **grilling/direct medium-high heat** for 3–5 minutes more, with the lid closed, until the crust is golden and crisp and the cheese is melted. Transfer to a chopping board, cut into wedges and serve warm.

8 Use a silicone pastry brush to brush off any flour left on the pizza stone. Make another flatbread with the remaining ingredients.

MAKES: two 30-cm/12-inch flatbreads

TOMATO-BASIL FOCACCIA

PREP TIME: 25 minutes
GRILLING TIME: 10–14 minutes
SPECIAL EQUIPMENT: rectangular pizza stone

750 g/1½ lb Pizza Dough (for recipe, see page 142)
Plain flour
1½ tablespoons extra-virgin olive oil, plus more for serving
2 ripe tomatoes, each about 175 g/6 oz, cored, deseeded and cut into 8-mm/⅓-inch dice
1¼ teaspoons coarse sea salt
1 teaspoon dried oregano
50 g/2 oz Parmesan cheese, finely grated
4 tablespoons fresh basil leaves, torn into thin strips
¼ teaspoon freshly ground black pepper

1 Prepare the grill for direct cooking over medium heat (180–230°C/350–450°F) and preheat a rectangular pizza stone for about 15 minutes, following manufacturer's instructions.

2 Place a sheet of baking parchment about 42 cm/17 inches long on a rimless baking sheet and lightly dust with flour. Place the dough on the parchment, and then press, stretch and pull the dough into an oval or rectangle about 37 x 23 cm/ 15 x 9 inches and 1 cm/½ inch thick (don't worry if the shape is irregular). If the dough is too springy to work with, cover with kitchen paper, allow to rest for 5 minutes, and then continue.

3 Dimple the top of the dough all over with your fingertips, and then brush with 1½ tablespoons oil. Distribute the tomatoes evenly over the top, gently pressing them down into the dough, leaving a 2.5-cm/1-inch border. Season with the salt and oregano. Slide the focaccia, on the parchment, on to the pizza stone. Grill over **grilling/direct medium heat** for 10–14 minutes, with the lid closed, until the crust is golden brown underneath and pale golden brown on top.

4 Transfer the focaccia to a chopping board. Immediately top with the cheese, basil and pepper. If liked, drizzle with a little oil. Cut into wide strips and serve warm.

SERVES: 4–6

PORTOBELLO PIZZAS

WITH MANCHEGO AND MINT

PREP TIME: 30 minutes
GRILLING TIME: 17–21 minutes
SPECIAL EQUIPMENT: perforated grill pan, pizza stone, pizza peel
(optional), silicone pastry brush

750 g/1½ lb Pizza Dough (for recipe, see page 142)
500 g/1 lb portobello mushrooms, cleaned, stalks and dark gills
removed, caps cut into 1-cm/½-inch chunks
Extra-virgin olive oil
1 large garlic clove, finely chopped
1 teaspoon coarse salt
Freshly ground black pepper
Plain flour
250 g/8 oz Manchego cheese, rind removed, shaved into
1-cm/½-inch-wide strips with a vegetable peeler
4 tablespoons roughly chopped mint

1 Prepare the grill for direct cooking over medium heat
(180–230°C/350–450°F) and preheat a perforated grill
pan for about 15 minutes.

2 In a large bowl combine the mushrooms, 1 tablespoon
oil, the garlic, salt and ¼ teaspoon pepper. Spread
the mushrooms in a single layer on the grill pan and grill
over **grilling/direct medium heat** for 5–7 minutes, with
the lid closed, until tender and beginning to brown, turning
occasionally. Transfer the grill pan with the mushrooms to a
heatproof surface and set aside. Preheat a pizza stone for
15 minutes, following manufacturer's instructions.

3 Divide the dough into two equal balls. On a lightly
floured work surface, using a rolling pin or your hands,
roll or stretch out one ball of dough into a 30-cm/12-inch round.
Lightly dust a pizza peel or a rimless baking sheet with flour.
Transfer the dough round to the pizza peel. Brush the top with
1½ teaspoons oil. Slide on to the preheated pizza stone. Cook
over **grilling/direct medium heat** for about 3 minutes, with
the lid closed, until the dough is golden brown and firm on
the underside.

4 Using the pizza peel, slide the dough off the pizza
stone. Flip and evenly spread the grilled side with half of
the mushrooms and half of the cheese, leaving a 2.5-cm/1-inch
border. Slide back on to the pizza stone and continue grilling
over **grilling/direct medium heat** for 3–5 minutes, with the
lid closed, until the crust is golden and crisp and the cheese
is melted. Transfer to a chopping board, season generously
with pepper, and top with half of the mint. Cut into wedges
and serve warm.

5 Use a silicone pastry brush to brush off any flour left
on the pizza stone. Make another pizza with the
remaining ingredients.

MAKES: two 30-cm/12-inch pizzas

PIZZAS

WITH ROASTED GARLIC, POTATOES AND ROSEMARY

PREP TIME: 30 minutes
GRILLING TIME: about 1¼ hours
SPECIAL EQUIPMENT: perforated grill pan, pizza stone, pizza peel
(optional), silicone pastry brush

750 g/1½ lb Pizza Dough (for recipe, see page 142)
1 large head garlic
Extra-virgin olive oil
⅛ teaspoon crushed chilli flakes
Coarse salt
4 small Maris Piper potatoes, each 50–75 g/2–3 oz, cut into
2.5–5-mm/⅛–¼-inch slices
4 rosemary sprigs, each about 2.5 cm/1 inch long
Plain flour
1 tablespoon chopped rosemary leaves
250 g/8 oz fresh mozzarella cheese, drained and patted dry,
thinly sliced
75 g/3 oz Parmesan cheese, finely grated
Freshly ground black pepper

1 Prepare the grill for indirect cooking over medium heat
(180–230°C/350–450°F).

2 Cut off the top of the head of garlic to expose the cloves,
drizzle generously with oil, and then wrap in foil. Place
the parcel over **roasting/indirect medium heat** for about
45 minutes, close the lid and cook until soft.

2 Remove the garlic parcel from the grill, carefully unwrap
the foil to allow the steam to escape, and allow to cool.
Squeeze the cloves into a small bowl. Add 2 tablespoons oil,
the chilli flakes and ⅛ teaspoon salt. Mash with a fork to form
a paste.

4 Preheat a perforated grill pan over indirect heat for
10 minutes. In a bowl combine the potatoes, rosemary
sprigs, 1 tablespoon oil and ½ teaspoon salt and stir to coat.
Spread the potatoes in a single layer on the grill pan and cook
over **roasting/indirect medium heat** for about 12 minutes,
with the lid closed, until lightly charred in spots and fork tender
(but not mushy), turning occasionally. Remove the grill pan and
potatoes from the grill and discard the rosemary sprigs.

5 Increase the temperature of the grill to high heat
(230–290°C/450–550°F) and preheat a pizza stone for
about 15 minutes, following manufacturer's instructions.

6 Divide the dough into two equal balls. On a lightly floured
work surface, using a rolling pin or your hands, roll or
stretch out one ball of dough into a 30-cm/12-inch round. Lightly
dust a pizza peel or a rimless baking sheet with flour. Transfer
the dough round to the pizza peel.

7 Spread the dough with half of the garlic paste, leaving a 1-cm/½-inch border. Top the garlic paste with half of the chopped rosemary, half of the potatoes, half of the mozzarella, half of the Parmesan and ¼ teaspoon pepper.

8 Slide the pizza on to the preheated pizza stone. Cook over **roasting/indirect high heat** for 12–15 minutes, with the lid closed, until the crust is golden and crisp and the cheese is melted. Transfer to a chopping board, cut into wedges, and serve warm. Use a silicone pastry brush to brush off any flour left on the pizza stone. Make another pizza with the remaining ingredients.

MAKES: two 30-cm/12-inch pizzas

153

DESSERTS

PEAR AND CHOCOLATE PIZZAS

WITH CRUMBLED AMARETTI BISCUITS

PREP TIME: 20 minutes
GRILLING TIME: 12–14 minutes
SPECIAL EQUIPMENT: pizza stone, pizza peel (optional), silicone
pastry brush

750 g/1½ lb Pizza Dough (for recipe, see page 142)
Plain flour
1 tablespoon rapeseed oil
2 teaspoons pistachio oil or walnut oil
1 teaspoon demerara sugar
¼ teaspoon ground nutmeg
125 g/4 oz plain chocolate, broken into small pieces
2 ripe pears, about 500 g/1 lb total, cut into quarters, cored
and thinly sliced, divided
25–50 g/1–2 oz amaretti biscuits, crumbled

1 Prepare the grill for direct cooking over medium heat
(180–230°C/350–450°F) and preheat a pizza stone for
10–15 minutes, following manufacturer's instructions.

2 Divide the dough into two equal balls. Cover one with a
towel until ready to use. On a lightly floured work surface,
using a rolling pin or your hands, roll or stretch out one ball of
dough into a 30-cm/12-inch round. Lightly dust a pizza peel or a
rimless baking sheet with flour. Transfer the dough round to the
pizza peel.

3 Brush the top of the dough with half of the rapeseed oil.
Lift the dough and quickly and carefully invert it on to the
pizza stone oiled side down. Cook over **grilling/direct medium
heat** for about 3 minutes, with the lid closed, until the underside
is light brown and firm. Using the pizza peel, slide the dough off
the pizza stone. Flip and brush the grilled side all over, including
the edges, with 1 teaspoon of the walnut oil. Poke holes all
over the dough with the tines of a fork. In a small bowl mix the
sugar and nutmeg. Sprinkle half of the sugar mixture evenly over
the dough and dot with half of the chocolate pieces, leaving a
1-cm/½-inch border. Slide the pizza back on to the pizza stone,
making sure the chocolate doesn't topple off. Continue cooking
over **grilling/direct medium heat** for 3–4 minutes, with the
lid closed, until the crust is golden brown on the bottom and
the chocolate softens. Remove from the grill and spread the
chocolate evenly over the surface of the crust. Arrange half of
the pear slices and half of the crumbled biscuits on top. Cut
into wedges and serve warm.

4 Use a silicone pastry brush to brush off any flour left
on the pizza stone. Make another pizza with the
remaining ingredients.

MAKES: two 30-cm/12-inch pizzas

156

FIG AND HONEY FLAT BREADS

WITH SPICED MASCARPONE

PREP TIME: 20 minutes
GRILLING TIME: 10–14 minutes
SPECIAL EQUIPMENT: pizza stone, pizza peel (optional), silicone
   pastry brush

750 g/1½ lb Pizza Dough (for recipe, see page 142)
Plain flour
1 tablespoon extra-virgin olive oil
½ teaspoon coarse salt
4 teaspoons honey, warmed slightly
2 teaspoons brown sugar
250 g/8 oz mascarpone cheese
4 teaspoons full-fat milk
½ teaspoon ground nutmeg
¼ teaspoon ground cinnamon
300 g/10 oz dried figs, diced
Fresh whole mint leaves

1 Prepare the grill for direct cooking over medium heat (180–230°C/350–450°F) and preheat a pizza stone for 10–15 minutes, following manufacturer's instructions.

2 Divide the dough into two equal balls. Cover one with a towel until ready to use. On a lightly floured work surface, using a rolling pin or your hands, roll or stretch out one ball of dough into a 30-cm/12-inch round. Lightly dust a pizza peel or a rimless baking sheet with flour. Transfer the dough round to the pizza peel.

3 Brush the top of the dough with half the olive oil and season evenly with ¼ teaspoon of the salt. Lift the dough and quickly and carefully invert it on to the pizza stone oiled side down. Cook over **grilling/direct medium heat** for about 3 minutes, with the lid closed, until the underside is light brown and firm. Using the pizza peel, slide the dough off the pizza stone. Flip and brush the grilled side with 2 teaspoons of the warm honey and sprinkle with 1 teaspoon of the sugar. Slide the pizza back on to the pizza stone and continue grilling over **grilling/direct medium heat** for 3–4 minutes, with the lid closed, until the bottom of the crust is golden brown. Transfer the flatbread to a large chopping board.

4 Mix the mascarpone and milk, stirring to loosen, and then spread the flatbread evenly with half of the mixture, leaving a 1-cm/½-inch border. Top with ¼ teaspoon of the nutmeg, ⅛ teaspoon of the cinnamon, half of the figs and a few whole mint leaves. Cut into wedges and serve warm.

5 Use a silicone pastry brush to brush off any flour left on the pizza stone. Make another flatbread with the remaining ingredients.

MAKES: two 30-cm/12-inch flatbreads

APPLE TARTE TATIN

WITH CALVADOS WHIPPED CREAM

PREP TIME: 45 minutes
CHILLING TIME: 2 hours
GRILLING TIME: 20–22 minutes
SPECIAL EQUIPMENT: 25-cm/10-inch cast-iron frying pan

PASTRY

200 g/7 oz plain flour
3 tablespoons granulated sugar
½ teaspoon coarse salt
175 g/6 oz chilled unsalted butter, cut into 1-cm/½-inch cubes
75 ml/3 fl oz soured cream

FILLING

125 g/4 oz unsalted butter, cut into 4 pieces
150 g/5 oz plus 2 tablespoons granulated sugar
6 large apples, such as Granny Smith, peeled, halved lengthways
    and cored
1 teaspoon ground cinnamon
1 egg, lightly beaten

250 ml/8 fl oz whipping cream
1 tablespoon granulated sugar
2 teaspoons Calvados

1 In the bowl of a food processor combine the flour, sugar and salt. Pulse once or twice to blend. Add the butter and pulse eight to ten times until the butter is the size of peas. Add the soured cream and pulse four to six times until moist clumps form. Gather the dough into a ball and flatten into a 15-cm/6-inch disk. Wrap in clingfilm and refrigerate for 2 hours.

2 Prepare the grill for indirect cooking over medium-high heat (as close to 200°C/400°F as possible). Meanwhile, prepare the filling.

3 Arrange the butter in the bottom of a 25-cm/10-inch cast-iron frying pan. Sprinkle 150 g/5 oz of the sugar evenly over the butter and the bottom of the pan. Place the pan on your stovetop over medium heat and cook for about 2 minutes, until the butter is melted, the sugar is partially dissolved, and the mixture is bubbling. Remove the pan from the heat and arrange the apples, cut side up, closely together in the pan. If necessary, cut the remaining apples into quarters to fill in the spaces. Sprinkle the apples with the remaining 2 tablespoons sugar and the cinnamon. Return the pan to the stovetop over a medium-high heat and boil for about 20 minutes, until a thick amber-coloured syrup forms, rotating the pan occasionally.

4 While the apples are cooking, roll out the pastry on baking parchment into a circular shape to fit the size of pan.

5 When the apples are ready, remove the pan from the heat. Working quickly, lay the pastry over the apples and peel away the parchment (the heat from the apples will begin to melt the pastry). Tuck the pastry into the sides of the pan if there is some overlay. Cut three to four slits in the pastry and evenly brush with the egg wash.

6 Place the pan over **roasting/indirect medium-high heat**, close the lid, and cook for 20–22 minutes, until the pastry is deep golden brown and firm when tapped and the caramel is a deep amber colour. Remove the pan from the grill and cool on a rack for 1 minute. Gently loosen the edge of the pastry around the pan with a thin spatula. Place a heatproof serving plate over the pan. Wearing oven mitts, quickly invert the tart on to the plate. Allow the tart to cool slightly.

7 In a bowl beat the whipping cream and sugar until soft peaks form. Add the Calvados and continue to beat for 1 minute more.

8 Serve the tart warm, or at room temperature if preferred, with whipped cream.

SERVES: 8

159

APPLES

WITH VANILLA CRÈME FRAÎCHE AND TOASTED ALMONDS

PREP TIME: 15 minutes
GRILLING TIME: 4–5 minutes

4 tablespoons flaked almonds
1½ teaspoons honey
175 ml/6 fl oz chilled crème fraîche
1 vanilla pod
4 large, sweet apples, such as Gala, each 250–275 g/8–9 oz
Rapeseed oil
¼ teaspoon ground nutmeg

1 In a small, dry frying pan over a medium heat, toast the almonds for 3–4 minutes, until golden brown, stirring often and watching carefully to prevent burning. Immediately transfer to a plate to stop cooking.

2 In a small bowl mix the honey and crème fraîche. Carefully split the vanilla pod down the centre with a small, sharp knife, and scrape all the seeds from the inside of each half and add to the crème fraîche. Whisk to blend.

3 Prepare the grill for direct cooking over medium-high heat (200–260°C/400–550°F).

4 Core the apples, and then cut each one crossways into 1-cm/½-inch-thick slices. Lightly coat the slices on both sides with oil and season evenly with nutmeg. Grill the apple slices over **grilling/direct medium-high heat** for 4–5 minutes, with the lid closed, until softened and marked by the grill, turning once.

5 Divide the apple slices among serving plates, overlapping the slices slightly, and top with a generous dollop of crème fraîche and a small scoop of toasted almonds.

SERVES: 4–6

160

PEARS

WITH HAZELNUT STREUSEL AND WHIPPED CREAM

PREP TIME: 20 minutes
GRILLING TIME: 24–35 minutes
SPECIAL EQUIPMENT: 30-cm/12-inch cast-iron frying pan

STREUSEL

4 tablespoons hazelnuts
40 g/1½ oz plain flour
4 tablespoons porridge oats
4 tablespoons soft light brown sugar
¼ teaspoon ground cinnamon
⅛ teaspoon ground nutmeg
⅛ teaspoon coarse salt
50 g/2 oz chilled unsalted butter, cut into 1-cm/½-inch cubes

3 large, firm but ripe pears, each cut lengthways in half
   and cored
25 g/1 oz unsalted butter, melted
250 ml/8 fl oz whipping cream
1 tablespoon granulated sugar
½ teaspoon pure vanilla extract

1 Preheat the oven to 180°C/350°F/gas mark 4. Spread the hazelnuts on a small baking sheet and bake for about 12 minutes, until toasted and browned. Cool completely. To remove the skin, rub the hazelnuts in kitchen paper.

2 In the bowl of a food processor pulse the hazelnuts until coarsely chopped. Add the flour, oats, brown sugar, cinnamon, nutmeg and salt. Pulse once or twice to combine. Add the butter and pulse until the streusel is crumbly and resembles coarse meal.

3 Prepare the grill for direct and indirect cooking over medium heat (180–230°C/350–450°F).

4 Brush the cut side of the pears with melted butter, and then grill, cut side down, over **grilling/direct medium heat** for 4–5 minutes, with the lid closed, until lightly charred. Place the pears, cut side up, in a 30-cm/12-inch cast-iron frying pan. Spoon the streusel over the pears. Cook over **roasting/ indirect medium heat** for 20–30 minutes, with the lid closed, until the pears are tender and the streusel is golden, rotating the pan once or twice to ensure even cooking. Remove from the grill and cool slightly.

5 Whip the cream until it just starts to hold its shape. Add the sugar and vanilla and whip until soft peaks form. Serve the streusel with whipped cream.

SERVES: 6

PEAR FRANGIPANE TART

PREP TIME: 30 minutes
CHILLING TIME: 1 hour
GRILLING TIME: 1¹⁄₂–1³⁄₄ hours
SPECIAL EQUIPMENT: 23-cm/9-inch tart tin

PASTRY

200 g/7 oz plain flour
100 g/3¹⁄₂ oz granulated sugar
¹⁄₂ teaspoon coarse salt
125 g/4 oz unsalted butter, cut into 1-cm/¹⁄₂-inch cubes
1 large egg yolk
3 tablespoons iced water

FILLING

2 large, firm but ripe pears
2 tablespoons fresh lemon juice
125 g/4 oz granulated sugar
125 g/4 oz unsalted butter, softened
1 large egg
1 large egg yolk
125 g/4 oz almond flour (almond meal)
2 tablespoons pear brandy
1 teaspoon pure vanilla extract
¹⁄₂ teaspoon pure almond extract

GLAZE

100 g/3¹⁄₂ oz apricot jam
1 tablespoon water

1 In a food processor combine the flour, sugar and salt. Pulse one or two times to blend. Add the butter and pulse 15–18 times, until the dough resembles coarse meal. Add the egg yolk and pulse about eight times, until moist clumps form. Add the water and pulse about six times,until the dough begins to stick together. Turn the dough into a 23-cm/9-inch tart tin. Gently press evenly over the bottom and up the sides without overworking the dough. Using a fork, prick the dough about eight times. Refrigerate for 1 hour.

2 Prepare the grill for indirect cooking over medium heat (as close to 190°C/375°F as possible).

3 Butter a piece of aluminium foil and press, buttered side down, on to the pastry case and up the sides. Grill over **roasting/indirect medium heat** for about 20 minutes, with the lid closed, until the crust is lightly browned.

4 Peel the pears, cut them in half, and cut out the core and stalks. Starting from 2.5 cm/1 inch below the top of the pear, cut each half lengthways into 5-mm/¹⁄₄-inch slices, maintaining the pear shape. Lightly sprinkle with the lemon juice.

5 In the bowl of an electric mixer cream the sugar and butter until light and fluffy. Beat in the egg and egg yolk. Add the almond meal, brandy, vanilla and almond extracts and mix to combine without overmixing. Spread the filling in the bottom of the pastry case. Arrange each pear half over the filling, cut side down, in a spoke pattern, beginning in the centre with the tip of the pear and slightly fanning the slices. Gently press the pears into the filling.

6 Bake the tart over **roasting/indirect medium heat**, for 1 hour 10 minutes–1½ hours, with the lid closed, until the filling is set and golden. During the last 10 minutes of baking time, combine the glaze ingredients in a small saucepan and cook over a medium-low heat until the jam liquefies, stirring frequently. Push the preserves through a fine-mesh sieve into a small bowl.

7 Remove the tart from the grill and transfer to a rack. Brush the glaze over the top of the entire tart, being sure to glaze the pears thoroughly. Let the tart cool in the tin. Cut into wedges and serve slightly warm or at room temperature.

SERVES: 8–10

ORANGE-ALMOND OLIVE OIL CAKE

PREP TIME: 25 minutes
GRILLING TIME: about 40 minutes
SPECIAL EQUIPMENT: 23-cm/9-inch springform tin

Extra-virgin olive oil
4 large eggs
200 g/7 oz plus 3 tablespoons granulated sugar
1½ tablespoons finely grated orange zest
170 ml/6 fl oz fresh orange juice
1 teaspoon pure vanilla extract
200 g/7 oz plain flour
100 g/3½ oz almond flour (almond meal)
1½ teaspoons baking powder
1 teaspoon bicarbonate of soda
1 teaspoon coarse salt
½ teaspoon ground cardamom
Icing sugar (optional)

1 Prepare the grill for indirect cooking over medium heat (as close to 180°C/350°F as possible). Grease a 23-cm/9-inch springform tin with oil and line the bottom with baking parchment.

2 In the bowl of a stand mixer combine 125 ml/4 fl oz oil, the eggs, 200 g/7 oz of the sugar, the orange zest, 125 ml/4 fl oz of the orange juice and vanilla. Beat until combined.

3 In a bowl whisk the flour, almond flour, baking powder, bicarbonate of soda, salt and cardamom. Add the dry ingredients to the wet ingredients, beating to thoroughly combine without overmixing. Pour into the prepared tin. Grill over **roasting/indirect medium heat** for about 40 minutes, with the lid closed, until the cake is golden brown and a skewer inserted into the centre comes out clean.

4 Meanwhile, in a small saucepan combine the remaining 3 tablespoons sugar and the remaining orange juice. Cook over a medium heat for 2–3 minutes, until the sugar is dissolved and the mixture has a syrup consistency, stirring frequently.

5 When the cake is done, remove from the grill and brush the top with some of the syrup. Cool for 10 minutes in the tin, and then remove the cake from the tin and brush the sides with the remaining syrup. Cool completely on a rack. The cake may be wrapped in clingfilm and stored at room temperature for up to 2 days. If liked, sift some icing sugar over the top before serving.

SERVES: 8

ROASTED ORANGES

WITH OUZO OVER ICE CREAM

PREP TIME: 10 minutes
GRILLING TIME: about 15 minutes

4 oranges, about 1.4 kg/2¾ lb total
4 tablespoons ouzo or other anise-flavoured liqueur
8 teaspoons demerara sugar
½ teaspoon ground cinnamon
2 tablespoons unsalted butter
4 scoops vanilla or chocolate ice cream

1 Prepare the grill for indirect cooking over medium-high heat (200–230°C/400–450°F).

2 Cut four 30-cm/12-inch squares of aluminium foil. Cut off the top and bottom of one orange to provide a level surface. Using a small, sharp knife, cut off the peel and white pith, following the contour of the fruit. Peel the remaining oranges in the same way. Cut each orange crossways into six–seven 8-mm/⅓-inch-thick slices, and then reassemble in its original shape. Place each orange in the centre of a foil square. Pull up the foil sides slightly and spoon 1 tablespoon ouzo, 2 teaspoons sugar, ⅛ teaspoon cinnamon and ½ tablespoon butter over each. Bunch up the foil into a bag-shaped parcel and pinch the top closed, enclosing each orange completely.

3 Grill the orange parcels over **roasting/indirect medium-high heat** for about 15 minutes, with the lid closed, until the sugar is melted and caramelized. Remove the parcels from the grill, and then pour the contents of each over a scoop of ice cream.

SERVES: 4

CHERRY CLAFOUTIS

PREP TIME: 15 minutes
GRILLING TIME: 20–30 minutes
SPECIAL EQUIPMENT: 23-cm/10-inch cast-iron frying pan

15 g/½ oz unsalted butter
375 g/12 oz fresh cherries, stoned
125 g/4 oz granulated sugar
3 extra-large eggs, at room temperature
250 ml/8 fl oz whipping cream
125 ml/4 fl oz full-fat milk
2 tablespoons kirsch
1 teaspoon finely grated lemon zest
1 teaspoon pure vanilla extract
½ teaspoon coarse salt
40 g/1½ oz plain flour
Icing sugar

1 Prepare the grill for direct and indirect cooking over medium heat (as close to 200°C/400°F as possible). Grease a 25-cm/10-inch cast-iron frying pan with the butter.

2 Spread the cherries in the pan and sprinkle with 2 tablespoons of the sugar.

3 In the bowl of an electric mixer fitted with a paddle attachment, beat the eggs and the remaining sugar on high speed for about 3 minutes, until light and fluffy. Add the cream, milk, kirsch, lemon zest, vanilla extract and salt and mix to blend. Add the flour and mix on low until just blended. Pour the batter over the cherries in the frying pan.

4 Place the frying pan over **grilling/direct medium heat**, close the lid, and cook for 5 minutes. Then move the pan over **roasting/indirect medium heat** and continue cooking, with the lid closed, until the clafoutis is golden and puffed, 15–25 minutes more, rotating the pan once or twice to ensure even cooking. Transfer to a rack and allow to cool for at least 15 minutes. Before serving, dust the top with icing sugar. Serve warm or at room temperature.

SERVES: 8

NOTE!

For best results, bring all of the ingredients to room temperature before using. If fresh cherries are unavailable, frozen may be substituted. Defrost and drain the frozen cherries before using. Fresh berries may be substituted for the cherries.

PLUMS

WITH BRANDY-ALLSPICE BUTTER

PREP TIME: 10 minutes
GRILLING TIME: 6–8 minutes

125 g/4 oz unsalted butter, softened
1½ tablespoons brandy or cognac
1½ tablespoons honey
Ground allspice
⅛ teaspoon coarse salt
4 large, ripe plums, each cut in half
Rapeseed oil

1 Prepare the grill for direct cooking over medium heat (180–230°C/350–450°F).

2 In a small bowl whisk the butter, brandy, honey, ½ teaspoon allspice and salt until smooth.

3 Lightly brush the cut side of the plums with oil, and then grill, cut side down first, over **grilling/direct medium heat** for 6–8 minutes, with the lid closed, until marked by the grill, turning once. Remove from the grill and mound a generous tablespoon of the brandy butter in the centre of each plum half. Dust the tops with a little more allspice. Serve right away.

SERVES: 4

NOTE!

Use any stone fruit that is ripe and available, such as peaches or nectarines if preferred.

GRILLED FRUIT COMPOTE

WITH ICE CREAM

PREP TIME: 15 minutes
GRILLING TIME: about 5 minutes

2 firm but ripe nectarines, each cut in half
2 large, firm but ripe plums, each cut in half
Vegetable oil

SYRUP

100 g/3½ oz granulated sugar
1 teaspoon finely grated orange zest
125 g/4 fl oz freshly squeezed orange juice
4 tablespoons fresh lemon juice
½ teaspoon pure vanilla extract
¼ teaspoon ground cinnamon
¼ teaspoon ground cardamom

Vanilla ice cream
Freshly ground black pepper (optional)

1 Prepare the grill for direct cooking over medium heat (180–230°C/350–450°F).

2 Lightly brush the fruit all over with oil, and then grill, cut side down first, over **grilling/direct medium heat** for about 5 minutes, with the lid closed, until lightly charred and beginning to soften but still firm, turning once. Remove from the grill and, when cool enough to handle, cut into 2.5-cm/1-inch chunks.

3 In a saucepan combine the syrup ingredients. Bring to the boil over medium heat, whisking constantly until the sugar dissolves. Simmer for about 4 minutes, until the syrup is slightly reduced and syrupy in consistency. Add the grilled fruit and stir to coat. Simmer for 5–7 minutes, until the fruit is tender and the juices are syrupy. Remove from the heat and cool to room temperature.

4 Serve the compote spooned over ice cream. Grind fresh pepper over the top of each serving, if liked.

SERVES: 4–6

NOTE!

Feel free to substitute other stone fruit, such as peaches and apricots.

SIDES

STUFFED TOMATOES

WITH OLIVES AND HERBS

PREP TIME: 15 minutes
GRILLING TIME: about 10 minutes
SPECIAL EQUIPMENT: large disposable foil tray

4 ripe tomatoes, each about 150 g/5 oz
Coarse salt
Olive oil
1 large onion, finely chopped
2 garlic cloves, finely chopped
2 oil-packed anchovies, finely chopped
150 g/5 oz panko breadcrumbs
4 tablespoons roughly chopped Kalamata olives
3 tablespoons finely chopped flat-leaf parsley
1 tablespoon finely chopped mint
2 teaspoons finely chopped oregano
¼ teaspoon freshly ground black pepper

1 Prepare the grill for indirect cooking over medium heat (180–230°C/350–450°F).

2 Cut 1-cm/½ inch off the top of each tomato. Scoop out the core and seeds and reserve 2 tablespoons. Season the inside of the tomatoes with a pinch of salt and place upside down on a plate lined with kitchen paper.

3 In a small frying pan over a medium-low heat, warm 2 tablespoons oil. Add the onion and garlic and sauté for 7–9 minutes until golden, stirring occasionally. Stir in the anchovies and reserved tomato pulp and seeds and cook for an additional minute. Remove from the heat and transfer to a large bowl. Add the panko, olives, herbs, pepper and ¼ teaspoon salt. Mix well.

4 Brush a large disposable foil tray with oil. Stuff the tomatoes with the breadcrumb mixture, packing it down slightly, and then drizzle evenly with 1 tablespoon oil. Place the tomatoes in the foil tray and cook over **roasting/indirect medium heat** for about 10 minutes, with the lid closed, until the bread crumbs turn golden brown and the tomatoes are tender. Remove from the grill and allow to cool for 5 minutes. Serve warm.

SERVES: 4

GRILL-ROASTED TOMATOES

WITH GARLIC BREADCRUMBS

PREP TIME: 5 minutes
GRILLING TIME: 8–10 minutes
SPECIAL EQUIPMENT: perforated grill pan

4 large, firm plum tomatoes, each cut lengthways in half, seeds removed
4 tablespoons panko or dry breadcrumbs
1 spring onion (white and light green parts only), finely chopped
3 garlic cloves, finely chopped
½ teaspoon dried oregano, crumbled
½ teaspoon coarse salt
⅛ teaspoon freshly ground black pepper
1 tablespoon extra-virgin olive oil

1 Prepare the grill for indirect cooking over medium-high heat (200–230°C/400–450°F) and preheat a perforated grill pan.

2 Place the tomato halves, cut side down, on kitchen paper and allow to stand for 5 minutes. In a small bowl use a fork to blend the panko, spring onion, garlic, oregano, salt and pepper. Stir in the oil and press the mixture with the back of the fork, blending the ingredients completely.

3 Fill each tomato half with about 1 tablespoon of the bread crumb mixture. Grill the tomatoes, filling side up, on the grill pan over **roasting/indirect medium-high heat** for 8–10 minutes, with the lid closed, until the tomatoes are warm and the breadcrumb topping is browned in spots (do not turn). Serve warm.

SERVES: 4

FARRO SALAD

WITH ASPARAGUS AND HERBS

PREP TIME: 15 minutes
GRILLING TIME: 6–8 minutes

Extra-virgin olive oil
2 teaspoons freshly grated lemon zest
100 ml/3½ fl oz fresh lemon juice
Coarse salt
Freshly ground black pepper
150 g/5 oz farro
500 g/1 lb asparagus, tough ends removed
25g/1 oz flat-leaf parsley, roughly chopped
15 g/½ oz mint, roughly chopped
4 tablespoons roughly chopped dill
75 g/3 oz feta cheese, crumbled

1 In a large bowl whisk 90 ml/3 fl oz oil, the lemon zest and juice, ½ teaspoon salt and ¼ teaspoon pepper.

2 Cook the farro according to package instructions. Transfer the hot farro to the bowl with the lemon vinaigrette and gently fold to combine.

3 Prepare the grill for direct cooking over medium heat (180–230°C/350–450°F).

4 Lightly drizzle the asparagus with oil, season evenly with ¼ teaspoon salt and ⅛ teaspoon pepper, and then grill over **grilling/direct medium heat** for 6–8 minutes, with the lid closed, until nicely marked and crisp-tender, turning occasionally. Remove from the grill and, when cool enough to handle, cut into 2.5-cm/1-inch pieces.

5 Fold the asparagus and fresh herbs into the farro. Top with the feta and 1 tablespoon oil. Serve warm or at room temperature.

SERVES: 6

ASPARAGUS

WITH PRESERVED LEMON AIOLI

PREP TIME: 20 minutes
STANDING TIME: 4 days
GRILLING TIME: 6–8 minutes

3 large lemons, scrubbed to remove any wax, and dried
2½ teaspoons coarse salt, divided
150 ml/¼ pint mayonnaise
½ teaspoon white wine vinegar
1 garlic clove, finely chopped
½ teaspoon freshly ground black pepper, divided
1 kg/2 lb large asparagus, tough ends removed
Extra-virgin olive oil

1 Fill a small saucepan halfway with water and bring to the boil. Using a vegetable peeler, remove all the lemon zest in strips. Juice the lemons and measure 150 ml/¼ pint juice; set the juice aside. Blanch the zest in the boiling water for 1 minute, and then drain in a sieve. Place the lemon zest in a clean, 250-ml/8-fl oz jar and add 2 teaspoons of the salt and the reserved lemon juice, pressing down with the back of a spoon to submerge all the zest. Cover with a clean, tight-fitting lid, and allow to stand at room temperature for 4 days, shaking the jar vigorously once a day. After 4 days, the zest may be refrigerated for up to 6 months. Rinse thoroughly and blot dry before using.

2 Rinse, blot dry and finely chop enough preserved lemon zest to equal 2 tablespoons. In a small bowl whisk the lemon zest, mayonnaise, vinegar, garlic and ¼ teaspoon of the pepper.

3 Prepare the grill for direct cooking over medium heat (180–230°C/350–450°F).

4 Lightly drizzle the asparagus with oil, season evenly with the remaining ½ teaspoon salt and ¼ teaspoon pepper, and then grill over **grilling/direct medium heat** for 6–8 minutes, with the lid closed, until nicely marked and crisp-tender, turning occasionally. Transfer to a serving plate and serve warm with the aioli.

SERVES: 6

RATATOUILLE

ON THE GRILL

PREP TIME: 15 minutes
GRILLING TIME: 24–28 minutes
SPECIAL EQUIPMENT: 25-cm/10-inch cast-iron or other grill-proof
frying pan

2 green courgettes, about 375 g/12 oz total, cut lengthways into
8-mm/⅓-inch slices
1 globe aubergine, about 375 g/12 oz, cut crossways in half, then
cut lengthways into 5-mm/¼-inch slices
1 large or 2 small red and/or yellow peppers, 300–325 g/
10–11 oz total, cut lengthways into 4 sections
1 onion, about 250 g/8 oz, cut crossways into 8-mm/⅓-inch
slices
Extra-virgin olive oil
Coarse salt
Freshly ground black pepper
2 plum tomatoes, about 300g/10 oz total, cored
4 teaspoons tomato purée
4 garlic cloves, finely chopped
⅛ teaspoon crushed chilli flakes
¼ teaspoon dried thyme

1 Prepare the grill for direct and indirect cooking over
medium-high heat (200–260°C/400–550°F).

2 Generously brush the courgettes, aubergine, peppers
and onion with oil and season evenly with 1½ teaspoons
salt and ½ teaspoon pepper. Grill the vegetables over **grilling/
direct medium-high heat** for 6–10 minutes, with the lid closed,
until marked by the grill, turning occasionally. Remove from
the grill as they are done. When cool enough to handle, cut the
vegetables into 1-cm/½-inch dice.

3 To a cast-iron frying pan add 3 tablespoons oil, the tomato
purée, garlic, chilli flakes, thyme, ¼ teaspoon salt and
¼ teaspoon pepper. Set aside.

4 Cut the tomatoes crossways in half, place a sieve over a
bowl, and scoop out the seeds over the sieve to capture the
juice. Reserve the juice. Grill the tomatoes, cut side down, over
grilling/direct medium-high heat for about 5 minutes, with the
lid closed, until shrivelled. When cool enough to handle, pull off
and discard the tomato skins, and add the tomato flesh and the
reserved tomato juice to the frying pan.

5 Place the frying pan over **grilling/direct medium-high
heat** and cook for about 3 minutes, with the lid open,
mashing the tomato flesh with a slotted spoon to blend it with
the other ingredients. Stir in the reserved diced vegetables and
move the pan over **indirect medium-high heat**. Close the lid
and cook until the mixture is just slightly softened (some of the
vegetables will still be crisp-tender), about 10 minutes, stirring
occasionally. Serve warm or at room temperature.

SERVES: 4–6

SMOKY MUHAMMARA

SICILIAN-STYLE GREENS

WITH SULTANAS

PREP TIME: 20 minutes
GRILLING TIME: 10–12 minutes

3 large red peppers
200 g/7 oz toasted walnut pieces
50 g/2 oz panko breadcrumbs
3 tablespoons fresh lemon juice
1½ tablespoons pomegranate molasses
2 teaspoons finely chopped garlic
1½ teaspoons smoked paprika
1 teaspoon ground cumin
1 teaspoon coarse salt
¼ teaspoon crushed chilli flakes
3–5 tablespoons olive oil

1 Prepare the grill for direct cooking over medium heat (180–230°C/350–450°F).

2 Grill the peppers over **grilling/direct medium heat** for 10–12 minutes, with the lid closed, until blackened and blistered all over, turning occasionally. Put the peppers in a bowl and cover with clingfilm to trap the steam. Allow to stand for about 10 minutes. Remove from the bowl, peel away and discard the charred skin, and cut off and discard the stalks and seeds.

3 Place the peppers, walnuts, breadcrumbs, lemon juice, molasses, garlic, paprika, cumin, salt and chilli flakes in a food processor and process until smooth, scraping down the inside of the bowl as needed. With the machine running, drizzle in just enough oil through the feed tube to create a thick, rich, smooth dip. Transfer to a bowl and serve with bread sticks, crisps or celery sticks.

SERVES: 8

PREP TIME: 15 minutes

3 tablespoons extra-virgin olive oil
2 anchovy fillets, rinsed and mashed to a paste
2 teaspoons capers, drained
1 onion, finely chopped
2 garlic cloves, finely chopped
¼ teaspoon crushed chilli flakes, or to taste
90 g/3½ oz sultanas
2 bunches Swiss chard, woody stems removed, leaves coarsely chopped
1½ teaspoons balsamic vinegar
½ teaspoon coarse salt

1 In a large nonstick frying pan over a medium-high heat, warm the oil. Add the anchovies and capers and cook for 30 seconds, stirring constantly. Add the onion, garlic and chilli flakes and cook for 2 minutes, stirring often. Stir in the sultanas and cook until they are softened, about 1 minute. Raise the heat to high and cook for 2 minutes, stirring often. Then add the chard, one large handful at a time, cooking until just wilted before adding the next addition. When the chard has all been added, reduce the heat to medium and continue cooking until tender, about 2 minutes more, tossing to combine all ingredients. Stir in the vinegar and salt and cook for 30 seconds, stirring constantly. Serve hot or at room temperature.

SERVES: 4–6

SWEET-AND-SOUR PEPPERS

PREP TIME: 10 minutes
MARINATING TIME: 30 minutes
GRILLING TIME: 12–15 minutes

4 peppers, 2 red and 2 yellow, each about 250 g/8 oz
4 tablespoons white balsamic vinegar
2 tablespoons water
1 tablespoon granulated sugar
½ teaspoon crushed chilli flakes
1 garlic clove, thinly sliced
3 tablespoons extra-virgin olive oil
2 tablespoons marjoram leaves, roughly chopped

1 Prepare the grill for direct cooking over medium heat (180–230°C/350–450°F).

2 Grill the peppers over **grilling/direct medium heat** for 12–15 minutes, with the lid closed, until the skins are blackened and blistered all over, turning occasionally. Transfer to a bowl and cover with clingfilm to trap the steam. Set aside for at least 10 minutes.

3 While the peppers are steaming, prepare the marinade. In a small sauté pan combine the vinegar, water, sugar, and crushed chilli flakes. Bring to a simmer over a medium heat and cook until the sugar is dissolved, stirring occasionally. Turn off the heat and cover to keep warm.

4 Remove the peppers from the bowl and peel away and discard the charred skin, stalks, and seeds. Cut into 1.5-cm/¾-inch-wide strips and place in a shallow bowl. Stir in the garlic. Reheat the marinade if it has cooled, and then pour over the peppers. Marinate at room temperature for at least 30 minutes. Stir in the oil and marjoram. Serve cold or at room temperature.

SERVES: 4–6

NOTE!

These peppers go well with grilled fish or chicken. They will keep up to 4 days in the refrigerator in an airtight container.

BASIL-PARSLEY TABBOULEH

WITH ROASTED PEPPERS

PREP TIME: 20 minutes
GRILLING TIME: 10–12 minutes
CHILLING TIME: at least 30 minutes

200 g/7 oz bulgar wheat, preferably fine grind*
400 ml/14 fl oz boiling water
2 large peppers, 1 red and 1 yellow
25 g/1 oz basil, finely chopped
15 g/½ oz flat-leaf parsley, finely chopped
1 cucumber, peeled, deseeded and cut into 5-mm/¼-inch pieces
2 spring onions, trimmed and thinly sliced
2 teaspoons finely grated lemon zest
3 tablespoons fresh lemon juice
3 tablespoons extra-virgin olive oil
1½ teaspoons coarse salt
½ teaspoon freshly ground black pepper

1 Prepare the grill for direct cooking over medium heat (180–230°C/350–450°F).

2 Place the bulgar in a bowl and pour the boiling water over it. Cover with clingfilm and leave to stand for 15 minutes –1 hour (*depending on whether the bulgar is fine, medium or coarse grind). Check package directions for amount of water and standing time. Drain and fluff with a fork.

3 Meanwhile, grill the peppers over **grilling/direct medium heat** for 10–12 minutes, with the lid closed, until blackened and blistered all over, turning occasionally. Put the peppers in a bowl and cover with clingfilm to trap the steam. Allow to stand for about 10 minutes. Remove from the bowl, peel away and discard the charred skin, cut off and discard the stalks and seeds, and then roughly chop the peppers.

4 To the bowl with the bulgar add the peppers and the remaining ingredients. Mix well. Refrigerate for at least 30 minutes before serving.

SERVES: 6–8

FUSILLI

WITH COURGETTES

PREP TIME: 20 minutes
GRILLING TIME: 3–5 minutes

500 g/1 lb dried fusilli
500 g/1 lb green courgettes, trimmed, cut lengthways into 1-cm/
    ½-inch-thick slices
500 g/1 lb yellow courgettes or pattypan squash, trimmed, cut
    lengthways into 1-cm/½-inch-thick slices
200 ml/7 fl oz extra-virgin olive oil
2 teaspoons coarse salt
1 teaspoon freshly ground black pepper
1 large orange pepper, chopped
75 g/3 oz feta cheese, crumbled
50 g/2 oz pitted Kalamata olives, each cut lengthways in half
4 tablespoons finely chopped mint
1½ tablespoons finely grated lemon zest
3 tablespoons fresh lemon juice
1 tablespoon Dijon mustard

1 Prepare the grill for direct cooking over medium heat (180–230°C/350–450°F).

2 Bring a large saucepan of salted water to the boil. Add the pasta, return to the boil, and cook according to package directions. Drain, rinse under cold water, and drain again. Transfer to a bowl.

3 Brush the courgettes on both sides with 2 tablespoons of the oil and season with 1 teaspoon of the salt and ½ teaspoon of the pepper. Grill over **grilling/direct medium heat** for 3–5 minutes, with the lid closed, until well marked and tender, turning once. Remove from the grill and, when cool enough to handle, cut into 1-cm/½-inch pieces.

4 To the bowl of pasta add the courgettes, squash, pepper, cheese, olives and mint. Mix the lemon zest and juice, mustard, and the remaining salt and pepper. Slowly whisk in the remaining oil. Pour the dressing over the pasta and toss well. Allow to stand for 15 minutes before serving.

SERVES: 8–10

LENTILS PROVENÇAL

PREP TIME: 20 minutes
GRILLING TIME: 10–12 minutes

200 g/7 oz puy lentils
1 aubergine, about 500 g/1 lb, trimmed and cut crossways
    into 1-cm/½-inch slices
5 tablespoons extra-virgin olive oil
1 teaspoon coarse salt
½ teaspoon freshly ground black pepper
1 red onion, finely chopped
6 garlic cloves, thinly sliced
2 large plum tomatoes, deseeded and finely chopped
50 g/2 oz pitted picholine or Kalamata olives, cut into slices
1 tablespoon capers, drained
15 g/½ oz basil leaves, thinly sliced
1 tablespoon red wine vinegar

1 Prepare the grill for direct cooking over medium heat (180–230°C/350–450°F).

2 Check the lentils for any small stones, place in a sieve. and rinse under cold water. Cook the lentils according to package directions. Drain, and transfer to a large bowl.

3 Brush the aubergine slices on both sides with 2 tablespoons of the oil and season evenly with ½ teaspoon of the salt and ¼ teaspoon of the pepper. Grill the aubergine over **grilling/ direct medium heat** for 10–12 minutes, with the lid closed, until tender, turning once. Transfer to a chopping board and cut into 1-cm/½-inch pieces. Add to the bowl with the lentils.

4 In a large frying pan over a medium-high heat, warm the remaining 3 tablespoons oil. Add the onion and cook for 2–3 minutes, stirring often. Add the garlic and cook for 3–4 minutes, stirring often. Add the tomatoes and cook for 2 minutes, stirring often. Stir in the olives and capers and cook for 1 minute. Transfer the mixture to the large bowl with the lentils and aubergine. Add the basil, vinegar, the remaining salt and the remaining pepper. Mix well. Serve warm or at room temperature.

SERVES: 4–6

CAULIFLOWER WEDGES

WITH CORIANDER GREMOLATA

PREP TIME: 15 minutes
GRILLING TIME: 12–15 minutes
SPECIAL EQUIPMENT: perforated grill pan

GREMOLATA
15 g/½ oz fresh coriander, chopped
¾ teaspoon finely grated lemon zest
⅛ teaspoon coarse salt

Extra-virgin olive oil
¾ teaspoon coarse salt
½ teaspoon paprika
½ teaspoon ground cumin
¼ teaspoon freshly ground black pepper
⅛ teaspoon ground cayenne pepper
1 small garlic clove, finely chopped
1 head cauliflower, 1–1.25 kg/2–2½ lb, leaves removed
Lemon wedges

1 Mix the gremolata ingredients.

2 Prepare the grill for direct cooking over medium heat (180–230°C/350–450°F) and preheat a perforated grill pan for 10 minutes.

3 Whisk 3 tablespoons oil, the salt, paprika, cumin, black pepper, cayenne pepper and garlic.

4 Cut the cauliflower, from crown to core, into 1-cm/½-inch wedges (some of the florets will break away). Brush the cauliflower wedges and florets on all sides with the spiced oil.

5 Grill the cauliflower wedges and florets on the grill pan over **grilling/direct medium heat** for 12–15 minutes, with the lid closed, until tender and golden brown, turning once or twice and reducing the heat of the grill, if necessary, to prevent over-browning. Remove from the grill. Lightly drizzle with the spiced oil and serve warm with the gremolata and lemon wedges.

SERVES: 4–6

GRILLED POTATO SALAD

WITH SPANISH CHORIZO

PREP TIME: 15 minutes
GRILLING TIME: about 18 minutes

4 large waxy potatoes, each about 250g/8 oz
1½ tablespoons sherry vinegar
¼ teaspoon saffron
Extra-virgin olive oil
Coarse salt
Freshly ground black pepper
1 large red onion, cut crossways into 1-cm/½-inch slices
125 g/4 oz cured Spanish chorizo sausage
½ teaspoon smoked paprika
4 tablespoons finely chopped flat-leaf parsley

1 In a large steamer basket set inside a saucepan over simmering water, steam the potatoes over low heat for 20 minutes. Transfer the potatoes to a large colander and cool for 10 minutes.

2 Meanwhile, in a large bowl mix the vinegar and saffron. Allow to stand for 20 minutes.

3 Prepare the grill for direct cooking over medium heat (180–230°C/350–450°F).

4 Cut each potato lengthways into four even slices, and then lightly brush with oil and season evenly with salt and pepper. Lightly brush the onion slices with oil. Grill the potato and onion slices over **grilling/direct medium heat** for about 10 minutes, with the lid closed, until tender and browned, turning once or twice. Remove from the grill and cut the potatoes into quarters and roughly chop the onion.

5 Grill the chorizo over **grilling/direct medium heat** for about 8 minutes, with the lid closed, until the fat begins to sizzle inside, turning occasionally. Remove from the grill and cut into half-moons.

6 To the large bowl with the vinegar and saffron add 4 tablespoons oil, the paprika, ½ teaspoon salt and ¼ teaspoonpepper; whisk to blend. Add the potatoes, onion, chorizo and parsley and toss well. Serve warm.

SERVES: 6

POTATO WEDGES

WITH ROSEMARY AND GARLIC

EMBER-ROASTED SKORDALIA

PREP TIME: 15 minutes
GRILLING TIME: 6–8 minutes

1 kg/2 lb large, waxy potatoes, cut lengthways into
    1.5-cm/¾-inch-thick slices
2 tablespoons extra-virgin olive oil
2 teaspoons dry white wine or vermouth
2 large garlic cloves, finely chopped
1 teaspoon finely chopped rosemary leaves
1 teaspoon coarse salt
¼ teaspoon freshly ground black pepper
1 teaspoon finely chopped flat-leaf parsley
Fleur de sel
1 lemon, cut into wedges (optional)

1 In a large steamer basket set inside a saucepan over
simmering water, steam the potato slices (in batches, if
necessary) for 8–10 minutes, until barely tender. Transfer to a
large baking sheet and pat dry.

2 Prepare the grill for direct cooking over medium-high heat
(200–230°C/400–450°F).

3 In a small bowl whisk the oil, wine, garlic, rosemary, salt
and pepper. Brush the potato slices on both sides with the
oil-garlic mixture, and then grill over **grilling/direct medium-
high heat** for 6–8 minutes, with the lid closed, until golden
brown and crisp, turning once or twice. Transfer to a serving
plate and garnish with the parsley. Season with fleur de sel
and serve with lemon wedges, if liked.

SERVES: 4

PREP TIME: 10 minutes
COOKING TIME: 1 hour
SPECIAL EQUIPMENT: charcoal grill, potato ricer

1 kg/2 lb king Edward potatoes (do not peel)
1 medium head garlic
3 tablespoons fresh lemon juice
1½ tablespoons white balsamic vinegar
1 teaspoon coarse salt
½ teaspoon freshly ground black pepper
125 ml/4 fl oz extra-virgin olive oil, plus more as needed
¼ teaspoon smoked paprika

1 Prepare a charcoal grill for direct cooking with medium
heat (180–230°C/350–450°F). Tightly wrap each potato
with heavy-duty aluminium foil. Cut off the top of the head of
garlic to expose the cloves, and then tightly wrap with heavy-
duty foil.

2 Lay the wrapped potatoes directly on the coals, put the
lid on the grill, and cook for 40 minutes, turning once after
30 minutes. Then set the wrapped garlic, cut side facing up,
on the coals alongside the potatoes. Put the lid on the grill
and continue cooking until the potatoes and garlic are soft,
20 minutes more. Remove from the grill and allow to cool for
20 minutes.

3 Unwrap the potatoes and garlic. Spoon the potato flesh
from the skins into a large bowl. Squeeze the garlic cloves
into the bowl. Push this mixture through a potato ricer into a
second bowl. Stir in the lemon juice, vinegar, salt and pepper,
and enough oil to make a thick, rich dip, spread or topping.
Garnish with the paprika.

SERVES: 6

CREAMY TWO-CHEESE POLENTA

WITH SHIITAKE MUSHROOMS

PREP TIME: 20 minutes, plus about 30 minutes for the polenta
GRILLING TIME: 10–12 minutes

POLENTA

750 ml/1¼ pints milk
350 ml/12 fl oz water
½ teaspoon coarse salt
175 g/6 oz polenta
75 g/3 oz Parmesan cheese, finely grated
40 g/1½ oz feta cheese, crumbled
40 g/1½ oz unsalted butter, softened

500 g/1 lb large shiitake mushrooms, stalks removed
1 red onion, cut crossways into 1-cm/½-inch slices
2 tablespoons extra-virgin olive oil
1 teaspoon coarse salt
½ teaspoon freshly ground black pepper

1 Prepare the grill for direct cooking over medium heat (180–230°C/350–450°F).

2 In a saucepan combine the milk, water and ½ teaspoon salt. Bring to a simmer over a medium-high heat, and then add the polenta in a steady stream, whisking constantly. Return to a simmer, reduce the heat to low, partially cover the pan, and cook the polenta for about 30 minutes, until tender and creamy, whisking thoroughly every 3–4 minutes. Remove from the heat, add the cheeses and butter, and stir until melted and smooth. Cover and keep warm.

3 Brush the mushrooms and onion slices with the oil and season evenly with the salt and pepper. Grill over **grilling/ direct medium heat**, with the lid closed, until tender, 8–10 minutes for the mushrooms and 10–12 minutes for the onion slices, turning once. Remove from the grill and coarsely chop.

4 Transfer the polenta to a serving bowl and top with the mushrooms and onions. Serve right away.

SERVES: 6–8

GRILLING GUIDES

FISH AND SHELLFISH	THICKNESS/WEIGHT	APPROXIMATE GRILLING TIME
Fish, fillet or steak. Includes halibut, red snapper, salmon, sea bass, swordfish and tuna	1 cm/½ inch thick	**6–8 minutes** grilling/direct high heat
	2.5 cm/1 inch thick	**8–10 minutes** grilling/direct high heat
	2.5 cm –3 cm/1–1¼ inches thick	**10–12 minutes** grilling/direct high heat
Fish, whole	500 g/1 lb	**15–20 minutes** roasting/indirect medium heat
	1–1.25 kg/2–2½ lb	**20–30 minutes** roasting/indirect medium heat
	1.5 kg/3 lb	**30–45 minutes** roasting/indirect medium heat
Clam (discard any that do not open)	50–75 g/2–3 oz	**6–8 minutes** grilling/direct high heat
Mussel (discard any that do not open)	25–50 g/1–2 oz	**5–6 minutes** grilling/direct high heat
Oyster	75–125 g/3–4 oz	**5–7 minutes** grilling/direct high heat
Prawn	40 g/1½ oz	**2–4 minutes** grilling/direct high heat
Scallop	40 g/1½ oz	**4–6 minutes** grilling/direct high heat

The types, thicknesses, weights and grilling times are meant to be guidelines rather than hard and fast rules. Cooking times are affected by such factors as altitude, wind, outside temperature, and desired doneness. The general rule of thumb for grilling fish: 8–10 minutes per 2.5-cm/1-inch thickness.

LAMB	THICKNESS / WEIGHT	APPROXIMATE GRILLING TIME
Chop: loin or rib	1.5 cm/¾ inch thick	**4–6 minutes** grilling/direct high heat
	2.5 cm/1 inch thick	**6–8 minutes** grilling/direct high heat
	3.5 cm/1½ inches thick	**8–10 minutes** grilling/direct high heat
Leg of lamb, boneless, rolled	1.25–1.5 kg/2½–3 lb	**30–45 minutes:** sear 10–15 minutes grilling/direct medium heat, grill 20–30 minutes roasting/indirect medium heat
Leg of lamb, butterflied	1.5–1.75 kg/3–3½ lb	**30–45 minutes:** sear 10–15 minutes grilling/direct medium heat, grill 20–30 minutes roasting/indirect medium heat
Rack of lamb	500–750 g/1–1½ lb	**15–20 minutes:** sear 5 minutes grilling/direct medium heat, grill 10–15 minutes roasting/indirect medium heat

BEEF	THICKNESS / WEIGHT	APPROXIMATE GRILLING TIME
Steak: rump, sirloin, rib-eye, T-bone and fillet	1.5 cm/¾ inch thick	**4–6 minutes** grilling/direct high heat
	2.5 cm/1 inch thick	**6–8 minutes** grilling/direct high heat
	3 cm/1¼ inches thick	**8–10 minutes** grilling/direct high heat
	3.5 cm/1½ inches thick	**10–14 minutes**: sear 6–8 minutes grilling/direct high heat, grill 4–6 minutes roasting/indirect high heat
Beef, minced	1.5 cm/¾ inch thick	**8–10 minutes** grilling/direct medium-high heat
Fillet	1.75–2 kg/3½–4 lb	**35–45 minutes**: sear 15 minutes grilling/direct medium heat, grill 20–30 minutes roasting/indirect medium heat
Kebab	2.5-cm/1-inch cubes	**4–6 minutes** grilling/direct high heat
Rib roast (prime rib), boneless	2.5–3 kg/5–6 lb	**1¼–1¾ hours** roasting/indirect medium heat
Skirt steak	0.5–1 cm/¼–½ inch thick	**4–6 minutes** grilling/direct high heat
Top blade steak	2.5 cm/1 inch thick	**8–10 minutes** grilling/direct medium-high heat
Veal loin chop	2.5-cm/1 inch thick	**6–8 minutes** grilling/direct high heat

All cooking times for lamb and beef are for medium-rare doneness, except minced beef (medium).

The cuts, thicknesses, weights and grilling times are meant to be guidelines rather than hard and fast rules. Cooking times are affected by such factors as altitude, wind, outside temperature and desired doneness. Two rules of thumb: Grill steaks, chops and kebabs using the direct method for the time given on the chart or to your desired doneness, turning once. Grill roasts and thicker cuts using the indirect method for the time given on the chart or until an instant-read thermometer reaches the desired internal temperature. Let roasts, larger cuts of meat, and thick steaks rest for 5–10 minutes before carving. The internal temperature of the meat will rise 5–10 degrees during this time.

GRILLING GUIDES

PORK	THICKNESS / WEIGHT	APPROXIMATE GRILLING TIME
Bratwurst, fresh	75 g/3 oz	**20–25 minutes** grilling/direct medium heat
Bratwurst, precooked	75 g/3 oz	**10–12 minutes** grilling/direct medium heat
Chop, boneless or bone-in	1.5 cm/¾ inch thick	**6–8 minutes** grilling/direct medium heat
	2.5 cm/1 inch thick	**8–10 minutes** grilling/direct medium heat
	3–3.5 cm/1¼–1½ inches thick	**10–12 minutes:** sear 6 minutes grilling/direct medium heat, grill 4–6 minutes roasting/indirect medium heat
Fillet	500 g/1 lb	**15–20 minutes** grilling/direct medium heat
Loin roast, boneless	1.75 kg/3½ lb	**28–40 minutes:** sear 8–10 minutes grilling/direct high heat, grill 20–30 minutes roasting/indirect high heat
Loin roast, bone-in	1.5–2.5 kg/3–5 lb	**1¼–1¾ hours** roasting/indirect medium heat
Pork shoulder, boneless	2.5–3 kg/5–6 lb	**5–7 hours** roasting/indirect low heat
Pork, minced	1 cm/½ inch thick	**8–10 minutes** grilling/direct medium heat
Ribs, baby back	750 g–1.75 kg/1½–2 lb	**3–4 hours** roasting/indirect low heat
Ribs, country-style, boneless	2.5 cm/1 inch thick	**12–15 minutes** grilling/direct medium heat
Ribs, country-style, bone-in	2.5 cm/1 inch thick	**45–50 minutes** roasting/indirect medium heat
Ribs, spareribs	1.25–1.75 kg/2½–3½ lb	**3–4 hours** roasting/indirect low heat

Official guidelines recommend that pork is cooked to 70°C/160°F, but most chefs today cook it to 63°C/145°F or 65°C/150°F, when it still has some pink in the centre and all the juices haven't been driven out. Of course, the doneness you choose is entirely up to you. Let roasts, larger cuts of meat and thick chops rest for 5–10 minutes before carving. The internal temperature of the meat will rise 5–10 degrees during this time.

POULTRY	THICKNESS/WEIGHT	APPROXIMATE GRILLING TIME
Chicken breast, bone-in	300–375 g/10–12 oz	**23–35 minutes:** 3–5 minutes grilling/direct medium heat, 20–30 minutes roasting/indirect medium heat
Chicken breast, boneless, skinless	175–250 g/6–8 oz	**8–12 minutes** grilling/direct medium heat
Chicken drumstick	75–125 g/3–4 oz	**26–40 minutes:** 6–10 minutes grilling/direct medium heat, 20–30 minutes roasting/indirect medium heat
Chicken thigh, bone-in	150–175 g/5–6 oz	**36–40 minutes:** 6–10 minutes grilling/direct medium heat, 30 minutes roasting/indirect medium heat
Chicken thigh, boneless, skinless	125 g/4 oz	**8–10 minutes** grilling/direct medium heat
Chicken thigh, minced	1.5 cm/¾ inch thick	**12–14 minutes** grilling/direct medium heat
Chicken, whole	2–2.5 kg/4–5 lb	**1¼–1½ hours** roasting/indirect medium heat
Chicken, whole leg	300–375 g/10–12 oz	**48 minutes–1 hour:** 40–50 minutes roasting/indirect medium heat, 8–10 minutes grilling/direct medium heat
Chicken wing	50–75 g/2–3 oz	**35–43 minutes:** 30–35 minutes roasting/indirect medium heat, 5–8 minutes grilling/direct medium heat
Duck breast, boneless	300–375 g/10–12 oz	**9–12 minutes:** 3–4 minutes grilling/direct low heat, 6–8 minutes roasting/indirect high heat
Duck, whole	2.75–3 kg/5½–6 lb	**40 minutes** roasting/indirect high heat
Turkey breast, boneless	1.25 kg/2½ lb	**1–1¼ hours** roasting/indirect medium heat
Turkey, whole, not stuffed	5–6 kg/10–12 lb	**2½–3½ hours** roasting/indirect medium-low heat

The cuts, thicknesses, weights and grilling times are meant to be guidelines rather than hard and fast rules. Cooking times are affected by such factors as altitude, wind and outside temperature. Cooking times are for the official recommendation of 74°C/65°F. Let whole poultry rest for 10–15 minutes before carving. The internal temperature of the meat will rise 5–10 degrees during this time.

GRILLING GUIDES

VEGETABLES	THICKNESS/SIZE	APPROXIMATE GRILLING TIME
Artichoke (300–375 g/10 to 12 oz)	whole	**14–18 minutes:** boil 10–12 minutes; cut in half and grill 4–6 minutes grilling/direct medium heat
Asparagus	1-cm/½-inch diameter	**6–8 minutes** grilling/direct medium heat
Aubergine	1-cm/½-inch slices	**8–10 minutes** grilling/direct medium heat
Carrot	2.5-cm/1-inch diameter	**7–11 minutes:** boil 4–6 minutes, grill 3–5 minutes grilling/direct high heat
Corn, husked		**10–15 minutes** grilling/direct medium heat
Corn, in husk		**25–30 minutes** grilling/direct medium heat
Courgettes	1-cm/½-inch slices	**3–5 minutes** grilling/direct medium heat
	halved	**4–6 minutes** grilling/direct medium heat
Fennel	5-mm/¼-inch slices	**10–12 minutes** grilling/direct medium heat
Garlic	whole	**45 minutes–1 hour** roasting/indirect medium heat
Mushroom, button or shiitake		**8–10 minutes** grilling/direct medium heat
Mushroom, portobello		**10–15 minutes** grilling/direct medium heat
Onion	halved	**35–40 minutes** roasting/indirect medium heat
	1-cm/½-inch slices	**8–12 minutes** grilling/direct medium heat
Pepper	whole	**10–15 minutes** grilling/direct medium heat
Pepper	5-mm/¼-inch slices	**6–8 minutes** grilling/direct medium heat
Potato	whole	**45 minutes–1 hour** roasting/indirect medium heat
	1-cm/½-inch slices	**14–16 minutes** grilling/direct medium heat
Potato, new	halved	**15–20 minutes** grilling/direct medium heat
Spring onion	whole	**3–4 minutes** grilling/direct medium heat
Sweet potato	whole	**50 minutes–1 hour** roasting/indirect medium heat
	5-mm/¼-inch slices	**8–10 minutes** grilling/direct medium heat
Tomato	halved	**6–8 minutes** grilling/direct medium heat
	whole	**8–10 minutes** grilling/direct medium heat

INDEX

An Hachette UK Company
www.hachette.co.uk

First published in Great Britain in 2016 by Hamlyn, a division of Octopus Publishing Group Ltd
Carmelite House
50 Victoria Embankment
London EC4Y 0DZ
www.octopusbooks.co.uk

ISBN 978-0-600-63249-8

A CIP catalogue record for this book is available from the British Library.
Printed and bound in China

10 9 8 7 6 5 4 3 2 1

www.weber.com® • www.rabbleandrouser.com
Author Jamie Purviance
Managing editor (US edition) Marsha Capen
Photography Tim Turner
Photographer and Photo Art Director Josh Marrah, Digital Guru
Food styling Lynn Gagné, Food Stylist Nina Albazi, Assistant Food Stylist
Editorial, design and production rabble+rouser, inc. Christina Schroeder, Chief Creative Director Marsha Capen, Editorial Director Shum Prats, Creative Director Robert Shearer, Photographer, pages 10 & 11
Colour imaging and in-house prepress Weber Creative Services
Contributors Lynda Balslev, Brigit Binns, Lena Birnbaum, David Bonom, Sarah Epstein, Suzy Farnworth, Elizabeth Hughes, Lesley Porcelli, Rick Rodgers, Cheryl Sternman Rule, Bruce Weinstein, Terri Pischoff Wuerthner
Weber-Stephen Products LLC Mike Kempster Sr., Chief Marketing Officer
Brooke Jones, VP Corporate Marketing
Round Mountain Media Susan Maruyama, Consulting Global Publishing Director
Senior Marketing Executive Weber-Stephens Products UK Helen Raison,
Director of Marketing Weber-Stephens Products UK Laura Ashall,
Director of Sales Weber-Stephens Products UK Jo McDonald,
Senior Commissioning Editor (Octopus) Eleanor Maxfield
Designers (Octopus) Jeremy Tilston and Jaz Bahra
Editor (Octopus) Pauline Bache
Production Controller (Octopus) Sarah Kramer